Harnessing the Power of Conflict:
Leading, Living, Learning
Third Edition

Resolving Conflict, Improving Relationships, Managing Change and Coaching Others

by

Norman C. Dasenbrook, MS, LCPC

and

Michael D. Mastroianni, MAT

C_S

Crysand Press

ABOUT THE AUTHORS

Norman C. Dasenbrook, M.S., L.C.P.C. is a Licensed Clinical Professional Counselor who has more than 25 years experience in the fields of mental health, consulting, teaching, business and alternative dispute resolution processes. He is a mediator in private practice concentrating on family, corporate and work group mediation, and works as a consultant and provider to numerous local and national Employee Assistance Programs and managed health care companies.

Mr. Dasenbrook has extensive experience consulting for businesses, industry, and health care. Lecturer, teacher and consultant to a number of corporations, He is a clinician who maintains a private practice in individual, marriage and family counseling in Rockford, Ill.

Michael D. Mastroianni, B.A., M.A.T. is Dean of Community Outreach at Rock Valley College, Rockford, Ill., where he directs the efforts of eight departments and more than 100 employees in all aspects of the college that touch the community. Formerly, he was a Principal and Human Resource Consultant with Management Resource Group, Ltd., a full service HR consulting firm with offices in Rockford, Ill. and Davenport, Iowa. In addition to his national speaking and consulting experience, Mr. Mastroianni also has served as Vice President of HR for an international educational association and has held key positions in health care human resources and in management.

Mr. Mastroianni is the author of a wellness program and a number of articles, including "Discipline In The Workplace Using Options Management," "Supervising The Problem Employee," and "Managing Multiple Priorities."

Mr. Mastroianni and Mr. Dasenbrook use their principles of harnessing the power of conflict with a variety of companies, service organizations, professional societies, health care organizations and hospitals. They are also co-authors of Harnessing the Power of Conflict: Optimum Performance Through the Self-Mediation Method, 1994, Crysand Press and Harnessing the Power of Conflict: Business and Family, 1997, Crysand Press. In addition, the two men serve as coaches for improving performance and interpersonal skills within organizations.

Crysand Press

3703 N. Main St. Suite 100
Rockford, IL 61103

Intra-group Mediation, and the Self Mediation Method are Trademarks of
Norman Dasenbrook and Michael Mastroianni.

Edited by Lincoln Brunner
Art Design by Sherry Young and Deb Strout
Photographs by Brian Thomas

Psychology, Business
ISBN 0-9643949-2-8

CONTENTS

Harnessing the Power of Conflict

"The Self Mediation Method"

PREFACE

PREFACE

By Norman C. Dasenbrook, M.S., L.C.P.C.

Harnessing the Power of Conflict is a culmination of our working with employees as supervisors, human resource personnel, Employee Assistance Program (EAP) providers, administrators, co-workers and CEOs. Before our collaboration, both Mike Mastroianni and I felt, but could not accurately diagnose, that a component to effective conflict management at the lowest organizational level possible was missing for many work groups.

I had worked with EAP programs helping "troubled employees," providing consultation to management on how to handle people, and running my own small corporation and private counseling practice. In my practice, I had observed that treating the problems at work was not always enough. We could trace conflict to its origins, diagnose individual and group pathology, help employees vent concerns and individually feel better about themselves, but we seemed to lack certain skills and an overall plan to settle future conflicts. We were able to settle disputes and treat individual psychopathology; however, the cultural change was not always occurring or long-lasting. Mike had risen through the ranks of various health care and private industrial settings from human resource training coordinator, vice president of human resources, acting CEO and finally business partner in his own full service human resource consulting firm.

Mike could teach people skills such as leadership, effective discipline, interviewing and communication; create action and strategic plans; and install teams, all with good success. But conflicts still were a major stumbling block. Some work groups were just unable or unwilling to let go of past problems or behaviors. Many reacted negatively to any corporate change, no matter how beneficial it potentially would be to the employees or the bottom line.

Working together, Mike and I found that we could combine techniques from organizational development, consulting and marriage and family therapy and apply those principles to work groups.

In the early '90s, one health care client asked us about conflict resolution for a unit that seemed very dysfunctional, wondering if the whole unit shouldn't be fired. Mike suggested that we apply the proven techniques of therapy to try to induce some change.

A one-day staff retreat was arranged. At the beginning of the session we asked, "Why are we here?" and BOOM!-it all came pouring out. The unit's employees were in conflict with management over pay and hours. They were upset with physicians, environmental services and medical records staff. And they weren't all that pleased with each other or the patients, either.

This group (like many others we've seen over the past 14 years) would not have responded well to individual or management consultation, nor would training in interpersonal relations have been sufficient to remediate their issues. They needed a cultural change and skill building to move into a different way of interacting more effectively.

We could feel the raw power of the conflict that needed to be harnessed, channeled and turned into a positive force. On the unit, a tremendous amount of energy was being expended to keep the group mired in conflict. We theorized that if we could transform half of that energy into a productive form, this unit could turn itself around and eventually handle conflict on their own.

So we decided to let them vent and facilitated their discussion on whatever they wanted to talk about. After two hours of venting, they began focusing on themselves, each other and their own problems. At that point, we asked them to break into small groups to rank their issues in order. Each group reported back with their top five issues which generally clustered around communication, trust, group problem-solving and conflict resolution. As a result, we taught them the skills they needed, including mediation skills, effective listening, assertive communication skills and meeting management and found they were eager and willing to learn. Having harnessed their anger into a positive force, we then returned to the specific issues. At this point, they were able to identify action steps and agree on how they wanted to interact with each other.

Reflecting on our experience, we saw that what the employees went through is not unlike what families go through in times of change. Whether that change is a result of birth, divorce, death, a blended family in a remarriage or any other external crisis, the process is parallel.

Moreover, as we continued to consult with employees regarding their work groups, family issues emerged. Since an integral part of the principles and techniques we use in our workshops and consulting practice are grounded in marriage and family therapy and mediation, we were able to encourage employees to apply the same principles to their relationships at home. Upon follow-up, employees reported improved relations–not only at work, but also at home.

Therefore, in the second edition of *Harnessing the Power of Conflict*, we have included concrete examples and anecdotes to help the reader apply these techniques at home or at work.

Upon reflecting on our experience, we learned:

1) Before you can be understood, you first must understand.

2) People need to be heard and validated to let go of the past.

3) Once people let go of the past, they are ready to move forward and learn new skills.

4) To practice new skills consistently, people need a plan with specific action steps and an agreement on how to communicate with each other.

5) Whether the goal is to help individuals communicate more effectively in a family or at work, the same principles apply.

We began to get requests from industry and health care clients to consult with work groups where the group itself seemed to be functioning adequately, but a key employee or executive was (or was perceived to be) holding the work group back. These highly trained (physicians, engineers, accountants) or highly placed (executives, managers, VP's) leaders were extremely valuable to the organizations and not easily replaced. So rather than work with the entire group, we began applying *Harnessing the Power of Conflict* techniques to individuals–with great success.

Thus, this third edition of *Harnessing the Power of Conflict* takes the use of our techniques in working with groups and families and applies them to the relatively new field of coaching. While the coaching profession in terms of sports is not new, coaching key individuals, executives and/or highly trained employees is. Coaching can take many forms but we define coaching as *a planned intervention with an individual to enhance or remediate skill sets necessary to optimally function or succeed in their leadership position.*

While all of the techniques of *Harnessing the Power of Conflict* can be used in coaching, we have outlined our coaching process in Chapter 10. This book is intended to help those coaches who coach, as well as those being coached.

This edition reflects our experience in refining this process over time, in working in a variety of settings. Keep in mind, it is a process not a solution. We have found that most people don't really want someone to solve their problems for them, although that's what usually is requested. Instead, they want a way to solve their problems themselves.

By Michael D. Mastroianni, B.A., M.A.T.

I have been lucky to work alongside Norm Dasenbrook with a variety of clients over the past few years. We have, in a sense, recreated and evolved what we do three times, hopefully to the benefit of the participants of our programs and to our mediation and coaching clients. The most recent makeover has been to extend what we have done in our work with mediation with groups and teams to coaching individuals one-on-one. When a person makes progress, it reinforces the importance of what we do and what people can do for themselves.

In previous books, Norm and I noted that in the mediation work that he and I have performed throughout the country, we found that more and more participants had concerns over issues stemming from the family *in addition to* issues from the workplace. Increasing requests for family role-plays were made to us.

Many managers ask employees to leave home problems at the door, and many families ask the employee to leave work problems at work. It is difficult to do either. People carry family concerns to the workplace and workplace concerns to the home. These concerns often produce stress and can affect the quality of the relationships at both places. As Norm and I often assert, the quality of work relationships directly affects the quality of products and services. Likewise, if things go haywire at work, it has an impact on the quality of family relationships, too.

Many people carry issues from home to work. If these issues do impact work performance, then something needs to be done to help people manage that conflict, as well. There is a great deal of transference in the work we do; that is, the same principles that we espouse for dealing with workplace conflict can be applied to the home with a few minor alterations. Since Norm is a Licensed clinical professional counselor with a practice in marriage and family counseling, we decided to utilize that expertise to provide the reader with methods for dealing with issues and conflict both at work and at home in the previous book. We still have those examples and information in this edition. A number of examples are provided for both arenas so that the reader can see how conflict can be harnessed in all areas of one's life.

It is our hope that this book can reduce the stress that conflict can cause and provide people with alternatives for resolving differences –alternatives that are positive and productive and that work in the home and at work. If these things can occur, then people will be free to do what they are meant to do: enjoy life, make a positive contribution to the world, work towards personal growth and get along with those around them.

What this edition includes that the others didn't is a section on coaching and enhancements to other chapters, including additional things we have learned from our continued practice. We have expanded on what we had before and added to it, trying not to change too much of the core content that is still relevant today.

We hope that the techniques will fit you, your family or your organization and that you have great results utilizing them in building better relationships and getting along with others.

There are many reasons why a person should be concerned with the quality of the relationships in their department or organization. When people get along, they are more content; and when they are more content, they produce better products and deliver better service. I recently went into a fast food restaurant. I asked the salesperson, "How big is your small cheese pizza?" She scowled and put her two hands together in a circle to show the size and said nothing. I sheepishly said, "Well, give me a small cheese." Thinking I wanted a slice and not the whole pizza, she rang up a price, shouted the number of the order in the microphone and told me, "Two-fifty." Knowing a misunderstanding had taken place, I said, "Two-fifty for a small pizza?" She scowled again and said, "You wanted a WHOLE pizza?" I replied yes. She then yelled in the mic, "Cancel that Bob, make it a #8", and then, frustrated, pulled the register tape, threw it away and rang up the correct price. She threw my breadsticks in a bag (I guess they came with the meal, but I sure wasn't about to ask).

Then I looked up at the wall. On a plaque was the name and picture of the employee of the quarter–and it was HER! I almost laughed out loud. Who *didn't* get the award if *she* got it? My guess was that the relationships were not that good at the organization. If they were, and she was happy, the service would have been different. Now, maybe she was having a bad day; I'd have to go back there to find out. But I won't. I wouldn't want to go through that again.

How many customers do you lose when your people act out their frustrations? It is important to take care of the interpersonal relationships and let other things take care of themselves.

I once heard someone tell the story of a trip he had taken. To keep his child occupied, he took a picture of the world from a travel magazine, tore it up into pieces and told the small child to "put together this puzzle of the world." The child had the puzzle put together in seconds. When the man asked his child how she completed it so quickly, the child said, "On the other side of the world was a picture of person, so I just put the eyes, and nose, and mouth where they were supposed to go."

The moral is to put together the person, and the world takes care of itself. These one-to-one confrontations, these small group mediations, these coaching sessions with a few key people influence the entire culture of an organization. The changing of paradigms on the top influences the entire culture. With industry in a bit of trouble, maybe the paradigms need to change. If a company is looking for bail-outs and rescues, for band-aid approaches to help the business rather than long-term solutions that may include diversifying, getting into different markets or product lines, or managing the people or culture in a more inclusive way with interpersonal skills in mind, then the short-term solutions will soon fail, too, along with the business.

Can we impact cultures, nations and the world by getting our act together and creating a positive effect on others, who then get their acts together? We think so. We think that is how you get culture change. We have seen it happen in our practice. We realize that no one technique is a panacea for all company ills, but there are some things that need to be done first. The processes mentioned in this book are first steps. Good luck in taking them. They will be the beginning of a journey that ultimately could change the world.

FORWARD

By Jennifer Cox-Baker, MA

In my work in the health care field over the past 10 years, I have witnessed a great deal of change and conflict in the workplace. I've often heard fellow staff members request (or desperately beg for) ways to deal with conflict both at work and at home.

I first became aware of *Harnessing the Power of Conflict* in 1995, when I was working at OSF Saint Joseph Hospital (a small community hospital) in Belvidere, Ill. I was serving on a committee that was trying to address some employee-relations issues.

Harnessing the Power of Conflict seemed to offer very useful tools that might help our staff "improve the quality of their working relationships." We decided to give it a try, and we invited Mike Mastroianni and Norm Dasenbrook to present their program to all of our employees.

Mike, Norm and their program were very well received. Employees greatly enjoyed attending the sessions, and we heard many positive comments from managers and employees as they utilized what they'd learned in the program both at work and at home.

In 1997, I began working in human resources at OSF Saint Anthony Medical Center (a 254-bed, Level I trauma center) in Rockford, Ill. I began serving on a committee that was trying to create a conflict/change management program for employees. We decided to turn to some experts for assistance, so we called Mike and Norm.

Our plan was to have one longer program for management-level staff and a second, shorter program for our employees. Mike and Norm led the program for management, which was extremely well received. Ninety-six percent of our directors and managers rated both the content of the program and the speakers as "excellent," and the remaining 4 percent rated them as "good."

For the program for non management employees, we asked Mike and Norm to bring their "Train the Trainer" program to us. We wanted some of our own staff members to be trained to present the program to our 1,900 employees, since we knew we would have to offer approximately 75 one-hour sessions to accommodate all employees.

Approximately 10 management-level staff members went through the training, which was very enjoyable and effective. Those staff members then led the conflict management sessions for all of our employees.

The results were overwhelmingly positive. Ninety-seven percent of employees rated the content of the program as "excellent" or "good," and 98 percent rated the effectiveness of the speakers as "excellent" or "good." Ninety-four percent said the program was directly applicable to their everyday work.

The written comments from attendees were also overwhelmingly positive. They included:

- The program exceeded my expectations.

- This applies to everyone.

- We need more inservices like this one.

- The program addressed questions and concerns very clearly.

- This inservice will help in many areas of my relationships at home and work.

- This really increased my awareness of attitudes and confrontations.

- The program gave me some perspectives not only on how to better communicate with co-workers but also with my teenager!

- We are dealing with many of these issues in our department currently, so this was very helpful.

- I have had real problems with conflict in the workplace, so this was great.

- It was informational and educational.

- Very useful and practical information.

- This will be helpful not only at work but everywhere.

- I work several jobs. I wish employees at my other jobs could hear this seminar.

- Very informative and helpful.

- It was very good, not only for work but especially at home.

- I feel more confident in approaching difficult situations.

- It has enlightened me on ways to have better communication skills.

- Learned several new techniques today that I will start using not only at work but also at home.

- Very good presentation.

- This was one of the best things I've attended. I attended this program once before, and it changed my life.

- Made me realize I have to think about situations before I react hastily.

- This information will be helpful in many areas, and even though I've heard the concepts before, the examples and reinforcement were great!

- It was much more effective than I had expected.

- Very good material and useful.

- Gave examples of how to get a working handle on confrontations.

- Very informative and eye opening.

- This inservice was so good, and the speakers were excellent and informative. They brought humor and caring to their discussion.

- It has been my goal to manage conflict better. This reinforces what I've learned before.

- It helped me understand people and myself in trying to deal with people.

- This was great because we need to learn how to deal with problems in a calm way in this type of job, because the patients are the ones who suffer if we don't.

- I have worked for other health care systems, and I feel that our management team really practices what they preach. This program impressed upon people that if you want things to change, you need to go about it with a cooperative attitude. I feel we really live that here. Other health care systems "dictate" to get change to occur, and therefore they get resistance from their employees. The fact that this program is being presented here shows that our hospital has an excellent management team. I am proud to be an employee here!

- This gave me a lot to think about at home and at work. I know I will be able to use what I learned effectively.

- Speakers were well prepared and spoke concisely and to the point.

- Seeing things in a different light helps you to think differently.

- With increased numbers of patients, it puts extra stress on us at work, and then conflicts increase. Therefore, this was especially helpful right now.

- I feel I could apply this to my work in a positive, constructive manner.

- All information presented was organized and clear.

- The role-playing demonstrations were especially helpful.

- The presenters were very knowledgeable.

- Excellent and very interesting. Great food for thought.

- Speakers were excellent and knew the subject well.

- Good, practical examples, and useful techniques.

Since that time, we have received a tremendous amount of positive feedback on the effects of the program on the hospital. Staff members often relay stories of how helpful the tools and techniques have been for them at work and at home.

Mike and Norm also trained some of our management team on mediation techniques. This has allowed us to serve as mediators for employees when they are struggling with especially difficult conflicts with co-workers.

I was one of the managers who received this mediation training, and from time-to-time, employees and/or managers will ask me to mediate conflict situations that they're facing. I greatly enjoy assisting our employees in this way. It's extremely rewarding to help two co-workers (or a group) break down communication barriers and work through conflict.

There is one employee I helped in this way whom I will never forget. She was struggling terribly with a co-worker, and finally her manager asked me to help mediate the situation. I did my best to help them, and by the end of our conversation, it seemed that we had made some progress. I told the two of them that if they wanted to discuss the situation further, they should feel free to contact me. I didn't hear from either of them for a few months, but the next time I saw one of the employees, she said, "Thank you! Thank you! Things are so much better between us now! We've not had any other problems that we couldn't work through together. I'm amazed and so grateful. Thank you!"

I pass that "thank you" along to Mike Mastroianni and Norm Dasenbrook, whose program has changed the lives of so many. We are constantly utilizing the tools and techniques of *Harnessing the Power of Conflict* in a wide variety of ways, and we are constantly reaping the rewards.

I wholeheartedly profess that their program has changed my life. I use the techniques on a daily basis both at work (in my current role as manager of about 250 volunteers) and at home (in my roles of wife and mother of a 2 year-old daughter.) Mike and Norm have truly taught me how to effectively work through and resolve conflicts while preserving relationships. I am tremendously grateful for the knowledge and tools that I have gained from this excellent program.

Jennifer Cox Baker, Volunteer and Senior Services Manager
OSF Saint Anthony Medical Center
Rockford, Ill.

Jennifer Baker is an independent consultant who has more than 10 years of experience working in the fields of marketing/public relations, human resources, training/consulting and volunteer management. She graduated from Northwestern University with bachelor's and master's degrees in business communication. She currently serves as the volunteer and senior services manager at OSF Saint Anthony Medical Center in Rockford, where she also helps coordinate their ministry development program. She also does consulting and training in the areas of conflict management and mediation. Jennifer and her husband, Randy Baker, have a 2-year-old daughter, Julia, and brand new baby boy, Daniel Johnathan.

Harnessing The Power of Conflict

CHAPTER ONE

Conflict Resolution, Mediation and Coaching

INTRODUCTION

Paradigms are models in our minds of how things should be. Some call them belief systems or perceptions. They are useful in helping us deal quickly with familiar situations, simple problems or minor concerns. They represent the way we always deal with things. When little is at stake, and we need a quick solution, relying on old paradigms might work quite effectively. But what if the concerns or issues are more complex? What if we haven't seen such a problem before? We then need to apply a more creative solution, and paradigms can block our ability to solve the problems at hand.

If you apply old belief systems/perceptions to new and more complex problems, the solutions often will fail. It doesn't matter how many times you try–if you are looking at a problem the same way you have looked at past issues, you'll probably not reach a desirable outcome.

For example, when your children were little and misbehaved, you may have been able to yell at them, send them to their rooms or take away a toy until they behaved themselves. Try applying the same solutions when they reach 18 years of age! They may yell back or laugh at you. If you try to take away something they bought with money they earned, they may refuse to give it to you. You can't apply a quick technique from the past; the longer you yell, the less they will listen, and the more you will feel angry, powerless and frustrated.

To solve problems and resolve interpersonal differences, you must change your belief systems/perceptions. The techniques of this book, or any other theory or practice cannot be effective unless your perceptions change, as well. The techniques proposed help you challenge your core beliefs and change them so you can adjust your problem-solving methods to each new and unique situation that arises. And problem-solving situations are all unique when people are involved, because all people are unique.

Why don't people appreciate what is done for them? Why don't they just let the new practices, policies or procedures work? Why don't they see it our way, even when it's obvious that our way is correct? The reason is simple: Everyone thinks that their own belief system/perception is correct. We all see the world through our own telescopes. If this is true, then it makes sense that we need to see through someone else's telescope before we can solve an interpersonal problem. We need to see how others view the world, what others believe, before we can solve a problem, resolve an issue or create an acceptable solution together. Therefore, we need to embrace what author Stephen Covey has written in the *Seven Habits of Highly Effective People*: that one must seek to understand *before* he or she can hope to be understood.

Many people mistakenly think that the techniques spoken of here are processes for problem relationships only. Although these processes are used to mediate solutions in problem relationships, they also can be used in other situations. When an organizational merger or acquisition creates a need to blend two different cultures, these processes can help. They also can be used in a downsizing situation that leaves the new corporate culture significantly different from the old, thus creating mixed feelings among remaining employees who may need some type of intervention to adjust to the new culture. When total quality management, continuous quality improvement, high performance teams, or shared governance is initiated, employees often have difficulty accepting the new empowerment philosophy–especially if they feel it is imposed upon them.

These processes can help in the transition. If people mistrust the core beliefs of the management team that initiates change, then mediation can be a remedy. If employees assume that management really isn't operating in their best interests, or they feel management is not committed to empowerment, mediation can assist. When the management remains autocratic or a growth occurs in an organization, and people need to get accustomed to new additions to the team, the conflict resolution and mediation and coaching processes can assist during that transition.

The processes also are effective at home and with friends. In a family, the ability to understand, communicate, solve problems and enhance relationships is just as important as in a business, if not more so.

Growing up, most of us did not intentionally study effective ways to communicate or deal with conflict. We learned from our parents, family members, friends or significant others who themselves may not have been the most effective communicators. Families, parents, children and spouses don't come with owner's manuals, and there is not necessarily a right way or wrong way to do things. As we grow and mature in life and in our relationships, we acquire our own styles of interacting with those closest to us. We adopt these methods mostly through trial and error, and they may be effective or not. We may discover what we don't want to do but not find what we want to do.

Sometimes it is more difficult to understand and communicate with those closest to us, because our feelings get in the way. The Harnessing the Power of Conflict Method gives us a true strategy or game plan on how to have quality relationships with others. But to make it work, we often need to change our belief systems or perceptions and look at things differently. When parents are trying to communicate with their teenagers, when couples are going through a divorce and trying to do what's right, or when divorced couples are trying to co-parent their children or trying to blend families together in a second marriage (having two sets of children and two sets of parents attempting to raise them), they need to re-examine how they are relating and be open to different ideas. By having a new understanding of why others feel and behave the way they do, families can develop a SHARED strategy that is healthy and nurturing for all.

It works! We have utilized conflict resolution, mediation, and coaching to resolve actual conflicts in the workplace in many different settings and industries. The techniques work between business partners, physicians, engineers, professionals of all types and for individuals at home, as well. We also have taught others how to use this process for themselves (Self Mediation).

In the chapters that follow, we will be explaining the processes of conflict management, mediation and coaching, their component parts, and how they can work for you. Perhaps you will accomplish what many have attempted—a systematic way of effecting behavioral change in a timely manner-by using the following five steps:

1) Understanding human behavior

2) Communicating/constructive confrontation

3) Using alternative dispute resolution processes

4) Establishing a code of conduct in business or a family contract at home

5) Establishing an action plan to ensure long term results

CHAPTER ONE

Key Points to Consider:

- Belief Systems or Perceptions are models that determine how we see the world and solve problems.

- The solutions of the past can't always be applied to the present.

- The Self Mediation Method can help people get along together.

- We need to see where the other person is coming from before we can expect our viewpoints to be understood.

Harnessing The Power of Conflict

CHAPTER TWO
Harnessing the Power of Conflict

AN OVERVIEW

Effective employee teams, families and key personnel function well because of certain qualities, some of which include not only communication, consensus and empowerment, but also disagreement. (Weiss, 1993). *Harnessing the Power of Conflict* attempts to foster both the qualities of effective communication and honest, respectful disagreement. It teaches people how to disagree.

Harnessing the Power of Conflict grew out of a combination of techniques from the disciplines of team building, group therapy, counseling, interpersonal communication, assertive communication, mediation and action planning. Blending or synthesizing these processes can be challenging–but very functional and productive if done correctly.

Many work teams, families and coaches have attempted to use these various techniques, but not necessarily as a comprehensive and coordinated approach. Some have had false starts when one or more techniques that yielded positive responses initially degenerated later. Things revert to the old, unacceptable ways of the past, much to the disappointment of all. Some have fallen victim to quick-fix attempts, with the same negative results.

TEAM BUILDING

In business, team-building techniques are productive in the beginning stages of team formation or development. Moreover, team building is a positive approach if the work group's problems are minor or not emotionally charged. Whether team building takes the form of attitude surveys followed by issue identification and action planning, outdoor training courses to foster problem solving and trust, or a series of exercises to foster group cohesiveness, the effects are the same; team building works well if things are not that bad. But these kinds of techniques cannot get to the core issues if problems are more severe.

When led by management from the work group itself, team building may be even less effective, because it is hard to be part of the team and lead the team in these sorts of exercises at the same time. Although the group members may feel better about what is happening for a time, the "lift" might not be sustained unless meaningful changes occur with strong commitment on the part of the leadership and the team members themselves.

GROUP THERAPY

Different forms of group therapy exercises can also produce positive feelings among work group members. Larry Pastor, M.D. in an article entitled "Single-Session Therapy Effective in the Workplace," points out the basic concepts for single-session therapy adapted from Talmon's book on the same topic. They include a "zeroing-in" on the most serious issue and searching for ways to improve. Concepts also include the need to search for ways to change, how to assess if change is effective and the need to be eclectic and have follow-up potential (Pastor, 1993).

The same can be said for Harnessing the Power of Conflict. The various forms of individual therapy adapted for groups help to produce the cathartic effect of getting things off people's chests within a peer group setting and help people feel accepted and validated by others. Normative behavior can start to emerge if a particular group meets on a regular basis, where members agree on how to interact and are unconditionally accepting of each other.

However, like some clients in individual or group therapy, some group members may drop out when they begin to feel better, because they no longer perceive the need to continue after the initial crisis has passed. As you can imagine, this often causes worse behaviors to emerge later. When a person does not take all of a prescription antibiotic, the infection may flare up and be worse than before!

COUNSELING/COACHING

Coaching is useful when a diagnosable mental health issue exists that can be treated with counseling or a combination of counseling and medication. More times than not, coaching is more appropriate, because coaching focuses on strengths and skill acquisition rather than symptom alleviation. It has been said the weaknesses are just overused strengths. Coaching can help give options and identify strengths.

INTERPERSONAL AND ASSERTIVE COMMUNICATIONS

Interpersonal communication and people skills are some of the most sought after skills in any environment. With constant change, people need the skills to handle change, communicate effectively and deal with conflict. Listening skills and the ability to communicate feelings and share ideas are critical to developing productive relationships. Without practicing these skills, however, people do not communicate effectively when conflict or anger arise. People may have the most impressive credentials from the most prestigious universities, but if they cannot communicate effectively, their ability to relate to others is greatly diminished.

Business and industry spend millions of dollars each year on employee assessments and psychological profiles, but these projective instruments and inventories cannot adequately assess communication and interpersonal skills. Just because someone is relatively free from psychopathology and is assessed to be a positive, future-oriented individual doesn't mean that he can communicate effectively especially in times of change and conflict.

In one organization, a department decided to implement self-directed work teams. With the administration sold on the idea, consultants were brought in to install teams. After three meetings, staff members were upset and arguing with each other while the process ground to a halt. Staff still felt the idea of teams had merit, but they had not developed the communication skills necessary to work on a team.

MEDIATION/ALTERNATIVE DISPUTE RESOLUTION

Mediation in business or family affairs has traditionally been employed to settle disputes among individual members, but not necessarily to resolve issues within a group. However, mediation has been helpful in achieving win-win agreements between labor and management, divorcing couples within families, small companies, or family owned corporations. The techniques also can be applied within work groups or families experiencing problems. Given that family mediation is a powerful method to help settle emotionally charged disagreements, it has tremendous power when the skills are transferred to the business setting.

One might think these skills must be assimilated by all those involved. Actually, not everyone needs to buy into the process or use the techniques. As long as some of the individuals use the skills on an on-going basis, the group still can undergo positive changes. The relationships cannot be like they were, and the positive changes will impact the whole group.

For example, in one group only three members out of 65 were negatively impacting the team. One individual was ignorant of the negative impact her extremely aggressive behavior was having on the group, another didn't care and still another was clearly an autocratic leader. Using only constructive confrontation, some–but not all–of the other team members began to confront these individuals when the negative behaviors occurred. After being confronted routinely by their peers, changes began. One of the negative team members became more cooperative and receptive to others. The autocrat was demoted to staff. The third person quit. Only a few were impacting the many in a negative way; conversely, only a few needed to use their skills to impact the many in a positive way.

Why did those three troublemakers either change or go? Primarily because the team members no longer tolerated their previous negative behavior. You may be able to ignore one individual who confronts you; it's a little more difficult to discount five or more who do the same.

Consultants, counselors and mediators can help settle disputes, but by acquiring the necessary skills, employee groups or families can mediate their own disputes. And relationships are nurtured and strengthened when conflicts are handled effectively. One cannot overemphasize the importance of strengthening the relationships at all costs. In the book, *Getting Together*, the authors emphatically state how important it is to do what you can do to improve the relationship (Fisher, Brown, 1988). What good is winning the battle if you destroy your relationships in the process?

Suppose for example, that you get into an argument with your teenage daughter about going out on a school night. You call her names and scream at her until she leaves in a huff and stomps into her room, slamming the door behind her. You open the door, tell her she is an ungrateful lout, ground her and slam her door on your way out. You won the battle; she won't be going out tonight. But what about your relationship with her? Have you done anything to nurture the relationship? Will she feel like telling you her problems and thoughts in the future? Will she feel like she can at least be heard and respected, even if you disagree and even if she doesn't get her way? Will she feel better about herself and her relationship with you? You won the battle and lost the war!

Stephen Covey speaks of how important it is to have positive interaction outweigh negative interaction. If we show discourtesy, betray trust and threaten our co-workers and family members, trust levels diminish. Then what do you do? Preserving the relationship is the most important reason to use the skills of this process.

ACTION PLANNING

Many businesses employ action planning, a process in which goals and objectives are identified, time lines developed and responsibility delegated. This tactic is most useful with homogeneous groups who believe in the goals and objectives and who communicate well with each other. The process depends on a task orientation and a religious adherence to action plans and time lines established by the group team. Action planning alone, however, cannot solve all the problems work groups encounter, because action planning does not foster the commitment to change often needed by groups to put their plans into action. But action planning *can* be an effective component in the change process.

Implementation of an action plan or any technique that imposes new structure quickly or without regard to people issues is an accident waiting to happen. Illustrating this was one organization mired in conflicts, disarray and lawsuits that brought in consultants to help the management team conduct action planning and brainstorm solutions to remedy their many problems. The first of two days was spent identifying issues and the second was to be spent in action planning to solve their problems. Some of the issues identified were lack of self esteem, lack of support, the society we live in, the legal system and lack of respect for rules and authority. These issues reflected the no-win positions that managers themselves felt they were in. Their personal feelings and an assessment of what they could and could not control were never addressed. As a result, on the second day, more than half of the management team gave excuses to the consultants and promptly left after the break. They realized that they felt helpless, and that action planning by itself was not going to solve massive problems they felt powerless to control. Instead, they elected to return to work, where they at least had some measure of control. The issues themselves were never resolved.

Action planning in the family setting also needs to consider people issues and timing. For example, as divorced people consider remarriage and how their blended family will develop, structure imposed too quickly can cause problems. The parents need to proceed slowly and involve all children, even those who may not be living in the family full-time. All affected family members need to be able to give input and offer ideas on how the new family could be arranged. Rather than saying to the children, "You really need to share your toys with Roger's kids when they are here every other weekend," the wife would be wise to ask the children, "In what ways could we help Roger's kids feel part of our new family?"

The previous discussions illustrate that one technique alone is not a panacea for all relationship ills. But all too often, a single technique is the prescription when a work group, family or executive is in trouble. Perhaps training is the answer; sometimes the lack of training or education is assumed to be the only reason the group or individual won't perform. We must keep in mind that just because people aren't doing what they are supposed to do doesn't mean it's because they don't know how. Sometimes they know how, and they don't want to change. Each technique has its usefulness, but when applied singularly, optimum group functioning rarely is achieved.

Optimum group functioning can be reached, however, when the participants are encouraged to:

1.　Verbalize and let go of past hurts.

2.　Identify current issues they can control.

3.　Learn how to control those current issues.

4.　Learn how to interact and communicate thoughts and feelings more effectively (something people used to think had no place at work) and then develop strategies on how to deal with other issues that may arise in the future, plan for what will be done and establishing a code of conduct on how to do it.

When these things occur together, the participants can deal with their problems effectively. Thus, Harnessing the Power of Conflict is a structured synthesis approach that combines proven techniques from a number of disciplines that are less effective when used individually. The overall conceptual framework of the process fosters healing, skill building and planning for whatever may arise in the future.

People often are looking for instant cures to their problems. Like aspirin, they want to fix the issues immediately. However, this process acts more like penicillin–it gets better over time. It may even get a little worse before it gets better. Sometimes people want to keep things the way they are because they have personal power when relationships are in disarray. They may not want to see things change; but as some people change, others will either have to change or they decide to leave.

CHAPTER TWO

Key Points to Consider:

- There are five essential steps in the Self Mediation Method.

- Disagreement can be healthy and build relationships if handled with skill.

- The overriding objective is to preserve relationships.

- A combination of techniques is more powerful than each applied singularly.

- Not all members of the family or work group need to change. If some do, all the relationships will be different.

Harnessing The Power of Conflict

CHAPTER THREE

COPING WITH CHANGE

Changing attitudes to get companies or individuals to change their behaviors is not easy. The only people we know who love changes are wet babies!

When most people change, they experience *change reactions*, which can include anger, stress, frustration, silence, blame and defensiveness. We label these change reactions THE MISERY ZONE because people feel miserable when they're going through it. When people bump into these feelings and responses, they would just as soon go back to the old way of doing things–in that manner, they can avoid the change reactions of the Misery Zone. The truth is, once a person is in the Misery Zone, she is almost ready to embrace the change! The Misery Zone reactions are signals that change is taking place and that the person already is incorporating the new desired behaviors. Being uncomfortable is a sign that it's working. If people remain consistent, the change will be long lasting. Others then will change the way they respond to you.

How do you cause the attitudinal changes that force people into the Misery Zone? By changing their belief systems or perceptions. Long lasting change seldom occurs without this. The following chapters provide information on how to understand perceptions and change perceptions in yourself and others and how to use techniques for effecting change in people you work with and live with.

KEEPING PACE WITH CHANGE

Changes take place rapidly today. Since it is difficult to react quickly to changing events, people need to be flexible and adaptable. It is also difficult to rely on past experience when trying to deal with problems, especially when they take place so rapidly.

Practicing what to do helps when the time comes that you actually need to do it. Those who train in the martial arts know that if you want to be able to block a punch, you had better practice it over and over again, until you don't even have to think; when the punch arrives,you block it automatically. The same holds true in other areas of life. We practice the coping skills we need to deal with conflict and problems so we can use those skills automatically when we need them. This helps us to deal with the changes that are taking place so quickly in our world today.

Some people get discouraged and say they can no longer rely on the traditions that used to get them by in times of stress. But traditions can be wonderful things. We cherish memories of past traditions. Grandma's house at Christmas. Going to the lake every summer. Family reunions over the 4th of July. The company picnic each August, complete with the softball game. When healthy traditions can be maintained, they can be a source of stability for a work team or family.

Unfortunately traditions sometimes change, too. Grandma dies. There's a divorce. The company doesn't sponsor the picnic anymore. But when these things occur, we can create new traditions. We'll still go through the Misery Zone; but on the other side, in the end, things will become easier, and we'll have the power to improve them. We'll be able to embrace activities and systems that will support us and our work or family group in embracing the new traditions and the changes that take place. For example, the people, places and things that support the new traditions can be a great source of help in establishing them as the new way of doing things.

When possible, of course, change should be introduced gradually. Daryl Conner, in his book *Managing at the Speed of Change,* points out that people deal with change more effectively when there are no surprises. He observes that people need to anticipate how others will react; how much commitment (or opposition) there is to the change; and how the family, company or culture will influence the final outcome (Conner, 1994). He also notes the importance of communication in the change process and how listening and producing trust helps people interact more effectively.

Despite our frustrations with them, changes will occur. However, interpersonal relationships do not have to be adversely affected by those changes. Instead, changes actually can strengthen our relationships, as long as we are prepared for them.

How can companies prepare for change? One thing they can do is **anticipate some resistance.** There will be less resistance if the change is planned and gradual, more if it is not. Resistance takes place because changes upset comfort zones. If we have to take a detour while driving home from work, it's upsetting, because it removes us from the familiar. How much more upsetting are work or family related changes, especially when they are extreme or sudden. It's difficult enough to deal with anger and resistance when changes take place gradually.

When change occurs at work, it may disrupt routines that we enjoy and that give us a sense of security. At home, the same holds true. When parents make sudden changes that affect the security of the children, resistance and anger are the natural by-products.

In corporations and in coaching, we often remind clients that when people act up and resist the change, it is probably working. We all want things to run smoothly, but introducing change will make things worse before it makes them better. With individuals who are attempting to change their own behavior in a coaching situation, there needs to be an understanding that people will not accept the new you automatically. It might take weeks or months of consistent behavior from the individual before the group accepts and agrees that the person is really different. If there was mistrust, it will take time to re-establish the trust again. It is difficult, but not impossible.

Effective leaders in the home or in business involve people in the change process whenever possible. Consider the typical work renovation project. A high-level task force is brought together, consisting of the builders and the heads of storeroom, plant operations, personnel, marketing, and administration. Meetings are held. Sometimes the manager of the department is left out of the planning and gets involved only at the end of the decision-making process. Each of those attending comes with an agenda and tries to make points protecting his point of view and interests. No one is quite sure what the other is going to do. The project is delayed because of changes that are being made by one task force member or another. The manager is angry because of lack of involvement in the process. She passes that on to the staff, who get frustrated and begin to set themselves up for disappointment. The builder gets frustrated from all the changes taking place.

Finally the project is completed. The refrigerator doesn't fit in the space designed for it, the wallpaper is ugly and no one thought about the need for a computer space. It may have been better if the company had a plan, if staff had been asked earlier for their input and if the manager had been a part of the design team from the onset–or perhaps if one person had been assigned sole responsibility to initiate changes with the builder. Leaders can be concerned with people and their needs, with the outcomes or with the overall goal; but they need to be sensitive to all of these areas.

Consider the parents who decide to pull their teenage children out of school to visit Grandma on a Palm Springs vacation. Once before when they pulled the kids out of school, they had been thrilled to go. Now, with no notice and no involvement, the kids are furious. They have tests to study for, friends they would rather be with, a dance they were planning on going to–and they'll have nothing to do in Palm Springs with Grandma. Perhaps some involvement in planning may have helped the kids, and the parents, deal with the natural response of resistance and anger to unexpected changes.

Consider an employee who is being coached who says that he tried what the coach suggested, and it didn't work. The person must ask himself, "Did I involve others or enlist their support? Did I try more than one time to affect the changes?" If the company or the family has an overall goal, if they involve those who will be affected in developing a plan of how to proceed, if they allow for as much time as possible to implement the plan and if they monitor and evaluate the results on an ongoing basis, then the change is likely to take place as smoothly as possible.

Families and companies need to consider the short- and long-term gains of the changes they wish to implement. What will be the costs in terms of frustration, time, money and people? Do the costs outweigh the gains? What would be the use of laying off employees if in six months there will be a shortage of people and the company will have a difficult time recruiting because they recently let people go? Why take a trip that will make everyone angry and frustrated for weeks afterward? Better to anticipate the negatives than to deny they may occur. People need to be overinformed rather than underinformed. When we know why something is happening and we're alerted as to what we can expect, we all can deal with the change better. Leadership cannot go wrong by dealing honestly with others. When people develop common goals, they can work with the leadership to ensure the success of the change. **With a shared vision that is communicated well, leaders can develop allies to help initiate and institutionalize change.**

If the leader educates or involves his group members, facilitates ownership and provides honest feedback, changes will undoubtedly take place more effectively. But most leaders also must deal with many factions and special interest groups, perhaps with conflicting desires. A vice-president tells the story of his days coaching Little League. Some kids didn't like him and some loved him. Then there was a group of kids who weren't sure. On the bench, the coach always seated the kids who liked him between those who didn't and those who weren't sure. Although simple, it made for a smooth-running season.

In a business, it makes sense to identify staff members with particularly good people skills and give them opportunities to utilize those skills in the change process. An employer may be able to identify staff members who are creative, innovative, communicative or diplomatic. These people can assist in the change process and be utilized as allies.

Care must be taken to avoid making expected outcomes self-fulfilling. Sometimes, people can develop a mindset (belief system or perspective), and then all they see is what they have programmed themselves to see. Our expectations or anticipations often influence the outcomes we get. If we're convinced that the neighbor kid has a behavior problem and is disruptive, then the only things we see are the behaviors that reinforce our beliefs. If we treat the kid as if those beliefs are true, the kid—tired of being treated like a criminal—may not disappoint us. Our expectations will bring about reality. This doesn't occur magically. But over time, those beliefs can become self-fulfilling.

Sometimes, a group will look at an employee being coached and develop a mindset that this person cannot ever change. Once that occurs, the coached employee may read this into interactions with the group and not disappoint them. On the other hand, a coached employee also may develop expectations of the group (how much they can achieve, who are the so-called good or bad employees) that can become self-fulfilling, as well. It is important to analyze how we communicate to others, verbally and nonverbally (smiling and making eye contact versus not giving the person time or even a glance when they interact with you); how and if we deliver feedback; how much we reinforce good behavior when it occurs; and what we tell people we think we can do. Even with our children, if we say, "Let Daddy get that for you, Johnny; I don't think you can handle carrying that in here without breaking it," you just told the child that he can't do it. Someone once said that we should substitute the words "I haven't found a way yet" for "I can't." In any case, people pick up what's expected and do exactly what they are supposed to do.

One of the authors once ran a 10K race. He had been training, achieving an 8-minute mile each time he ran the distance. When the race day came, he went by the first mile marker, and was notified that he did the first mile in a surprising 6.4 minutes! At the second mile marker, he had run two miles in 13.5 minutes. After he finished the race, he took his total time and divided by the number of miles. The result was an 8-minute mile. Because he thought of himself as an 8-minute mile runner, he had subconsciously slowed his pace after the first mile. That is how powerful our minds are and how self-fulfilling our beliefs can be. At work or at home, we must be careful what we communicate to others.

Changing ourselves is not always easy, especially since we've all developed habits. Habits are hard to break. This is because of *internal maintenance systems* that preserve our self-image of who we are and what we are like. If we want to change those images, we need to change our beliefs about ourselves. How to do this will be discussed in upcoming chapters.

Changing involves making decisions to change and acting on those decisions. It is an active, not a passive, process. Change is easier when we remove the forces that restrain the change and initiate forces that drive the change. We must initiate action and take away those things that pose barriers and create resistance. If the president of a company wants to transfer a key person to another state, an incentive of salary and benefits may help initiate the change, but the resistance factors (spouse likes job, kids like school, they all like the climate, they are involved in the local theater group) must also be addressed.

Change can seem negative and insurmountable; but with patience, it can be a process that revitalizes an organization or family. Since change cannot be avoided, it makes sense to use the best techniques available to make the change easier. Following the concepts of this book, we can minimize confusion, resistance and anger so our work and family lives can function smoothly. Change can take place from the inside-out or from the outside-in. We have all experienced outside-in changes ("I'll just throw the pack of cigarettes out and make myself not smoke" or "I'll make myself like her"). Initially, an outside-in change can work, but it is labor-intensive and hard to keep going. Instead of that type of change, or in addition to it, inside-out change works best. If we change what we believe, our feelings and behaviors soon will follow. Corporate cultures are merely shared belief systems. Corporate cultures can be changed, too. They are changed by changing the belief systems of the individuals within the culture. If the entire culture believes that management doesn't care about them and then management gives a 4 percent raise, they will view the change with suspicion and may say things like "Well, I guess they are trying to buy us off, but they can't fool us. They don't care." Unless the belief system changes, people will see only the things that confirm their beliefs.

Cultures change when people change how they view events. That means that we can't just keep quiet if we disagree with what someone says. That means we gently offer alternatives when people are looking at things negatively ("That could be true, Bob, but maybe they gave the 4 percent increase because they do care"). That means we use the techniques offered in this book to challenge the beliefs and attempt to change them–before the wrong beliefs become reality.

Always, people concerns must be taken into account to avoid disaster and confusion. We knew a missionary who once was confronted by a lion and dropped to his knees and began to pray. When nothing happened, he looked up only to see the lion with its face buried in its paws. The missionary said to the lion, "I'm praying for deliverance; what do you think you're doing?" The lion smiled and responded, "Saying grace before meals."

CHAPTER THREE

Key Points to Consider:

- Changes are difficult, and many people feel reactions to them and wish to go back to the old way of doing things.

- The new way of doing things becomes second nature if the techniques for surviving the Misery Zone are repeated over time.

- New traditions can be embraced to help people deal with change.

- Change should be introduced gradually, whenever possible.

Harnessing The Power of Conflict

CHAPTER FOUR
Communicating, Coaching and Leading

ISSUE IDENTIFICATION

One of the first steps in Harnessing the Power of Conflict involves the identification of issues. This is where the air is cleared and past and present problems, anger and resentments can be uncovered. Group and individual needs also are identified in the beginning of this process, which is much like the beginning stages of successful group therapy. In the first few meetings, group members often will state why they are there and what they hope to get out of the experience. This act helps form group cohesion around the common problem or concern that brought them together to begin with. Verbalizing concerns and having them validated by other group members and the group facilitator can have a healing effect. When group members are allowed to vent, they usually realize that others feel the same way (frustrated, burned out, unappreciated, depressed or angry, for example). Commonality of feelings and concerns are essential to the process.

One hospital requested our consultation in Harnessing the Power of Conflict for one of its nursing units because of an increase in patient complaints. The manager felt overwhelmed from spending an inordinate amount of time trying to settle disputes among the staff. After going over the introductions in the first session, we asked the staff why they were together for this meeting. Most staff members identified communication problems and personality clashes as the main issues. However, two staff members related that they thought they were present for an inservice training on closed head injuries! It definitely pays to ask what each person perceives is the reason for meeting rather than assuming that the reasons are apparent. It is important not only for validation and emphasizing commonality, but to clarify for the group the purpose of the meeting so that members immediately can think in terms of formulating plans to meet the group's needs. Likewise, when holding a family meeting, determine if each family member is clear on the purpose for the meeting; if they are unclear, clarify. Thus, the issues may vary from group to group.

While it is also important to let the group identify purpose and determine the need for change, it is important to pay attention to the process as well as the outcome. *Process orientation* rather than goal orientation is a key ingredient in the initial stage of issue identification.

Stephen Covey distinguishes goal orientation from process orientation with this illustration: If goal-oriented people are driving from point A to point B, they might look at a map and plot a course for the shortest distance between the two points. If process-oriented people are driving, they also would look at a map and plot a course, but their course would emphasize points of interest, rest stops and restaurants; and they may detour to other routes to enjoy the drive. Similarly, in Harnessing the Power of Conflict, we need to arrive from point A to point B, but the group needs to feel good about themselves while doing it.

In addition to group consensus, commonality and clarification of purpose, identifying issues allows participants to vent concerns and frustrations. Many organizations are fearful that this venting will degenerate into an uncontrollable gripe session, possibly raising issues that management may be powerless to deal with. Likewise, parents may fear a usurping of their authority by the children. One of the fears is that if the group ends up with unsolved issues, the members will be even more angry and frustrated than before.

One person in an organization asked that the Issue Identification phase be eliminated. She felt that management would be powerless if the staff vented. She had some past experiences with this, which resulted in frustration and ill will. But the issues exist whether one chooses to look at them or not. Management cannot be expected to solve all the issues; the whole point of Harnessing the Power of Conflict is to allow staff members to solve their own issues.

As any group therapist will attest, people can't move forward until they have let go of the past. If they miss this step, an important piece of the healing work of this process is lost. Group members need to feel that their thoughts and feelings matter; they need to validate them.

Venting or catharsis can take many forms, usually in relation to the extent of dysfunction in the group. The higher the degree of conflict, the more negative the feelings will be and the more need there will be to allow that venting. At work, staff members will not respond to a motivational program if they are filled with unvented anger and resentments. At home, if your spouse forgets your birthday on Thursday, you may not be in the mood to go to dinner on the weekend-at least not until your feelings are heard and acknowledged. Once that happens, you can let it go and have fun on the weekend. The objective here is to allow the venting and even to encourage it, if possible. When feelings are vented, the parties can let go of the past hurts and move on to the next step-setting up a framework to head off similar issues in the future.

Often when we ask, "Why are we here today?" the group will respond in a wide range of ways. Some groups or families will be angry about being called together, some will be apathetic and some will give a combination of issues and feelings. Others will deny problems. Common responses are:

"We are not the problem ... it's the_____department."

"I think this is a waste of time. Nothing ever gets better around here. We tried things like this before, and nothing's changed."

"The rest of us are looking for jobs...what we really need is a course on resume writing."

"This is going to be another waste of time. When management gets their act together and makes some changes and supports us, then it will work. We already had consultants in, and nothing is better."

"There's too much backstabbing and gossip. We aren't a team."

"Not another family meeting! You're trying to make us into the Brady Bunch."

If apathy or denial prevail, the responses will sound like the following:

"It's nice that the president is concerned for our team, but really ... we are doing just fine."

"I know we can always grow and learn, but I'm not sure why this training was scheduled."

"What's the use of bringing things up to you? You never listen to us kids anyway."

"I don't have any problems. His kids are a problem when they come to spend the weekend."

"I haven't the slightest idea why I am here. I got this memo saying that all the production staff had a mandatory meeting."

"If management feels we need the touchy, feely sensitivity stuff, they should have the meeting for themselves first and put the money they're wasting on you in our paychecks."

"I personally don't have any issues, but I hear others complaining all the time."

Moreover, if the groups' concerns are not well entrenched or emotionally laden, initial responses will usually mirror the following:

"We're not sure what to expect, but the atmosphere around here is pretty tense."

"The rapid growth we've experienced seems to be causing some turf battles, and some people aren't working well together. We need to learn to handle the growth."

"The downsizing has started to cause some cliques to form."

"What we need is to hire more staff, not have more training."

"Since the divorce, things are different; but I'm trying to cope with it."

If Harnessing the Power of Conflict is employed as a group enhancement methodology, used to make a good group better, responses also will reflect issues paired with feelings, such as:

"Things are pretty good. I mean, I like coming to work, but our department has some strong personalities that clash. When that happens, the rest of us run for cover. Sometimes, we walk around on egg shells."

"Out of 45 of us, we work well together by and large. There are just two or three that spoil it for the others. I know I won't say anything to them, because I don't want them getting in my face-nor do I want to cause resentment."

"I am not comfortable with this. If we share our feelings, it will come back to haunt us later."

"In this family, we can talk until we disagree with you, Dad; then you get mad."

Whether it is anger, apathy, denial or paired feelings, the issues need to be flushed out, heard and validated in an unconditional and accepting environment. The group should not be nervous about hearing such statements, and by no means should attempt to defend or dispute what is said at this time. Most of the time, the group itself will be accepting and validating as each member shares thoughts, feelings and concerns, as well as the issues. If the members can integrate with each other by listening, validating concerns and relating similar experiences, it is even better yet.

It is important in this process that group members truly listen. We know a person is truly listening when we see her being quiet, attentive, nondirective and able to paraphrase every once and a while what has been said. A good listener might look concerned, nod yes and make eye contact while commenting occasionally,

"I think what I hear you saying is _____ or _____."

"Sounds like your feeling _____ because of_____."

By allowing people to vent and move past hurt feelings from the past, the process of issue identification helps healing take place at the same time. Ideally in business, a facilitator from outside the organization conducts this process without the next level of management present. Parents also might enlist the aid of a qualified therapist or mediator. Sharing with outside facilitators is easier and safer for most participants, especially if the group has more severe levels of dysfunction. If Harnessing the Power of Conflict is used as group enhancement and the dysfunction is minimal, this is not always necessary; but the group should at least have the option of using outside facilitators.

Some groups have elected to keep management out of issue identification and include them in training so they hear the same information. If managers do attend, they should be grouped with other supervisors or managers during group activities, issue identification or role playing. If they are present at the start of an issue identification meeting, the management group should physically leave the room and come back for the sharing and recording portions of the program. This helps the staff feel more confident that the true purpose is to uncover issues without leader retaliation. To make the sharing even safer, the staff can brainstorm issues and problems in smaller subgroups with a person who writes down all the responses. In this way, no one can tell who made a particular comment within the subgroup. It must be noted here that many groups complete the entire process without management present to empower themselves to totally deal with their issues on their own.

TRANSITIONING

Transitioning is the process of moving away from a position of blaming people outside the group to a position of owning some, if not all, of the problem. Transitioning is very important: If the group won't own some of the problem, it won't be invested in attempting to solve it. Most often, the group will make the transition well from venting to identifying its own problems to taking ownership in them. Many times one or two participants will reframe the concerns into self-directed statements. The participants need to be listening for the transition statements and for what the core problem seems to be. Once identified, the group can move to the next steps. If these core issues are not identified and transitioning has not occurred, it is premature to attempt to move forward.

Transitioning statements sound like the following (take note that the core issue being identified is placed in bold print):

Issue: **Trust**

> "We are complaining about how the employees don't trust us, but I'm not sure we trust each other."

> "The kids say we are suspicious of them, but I'm not so sure we trust each others' judgment."

> "We get mixed messages from the supervisors. They say one thing just to keep us happy and then do another. As a matter of fact, I don't trust the others in this area to do what they say they will do, either."

> "The kids always say they will do their chores and don't do them; but how many times have we made promises to them that we don't keep?"

Issue: **Lack of Cohesive Mission**

> "No one seems to know what the hell is going on around this plant; but then again, we don't seem to have a plan for our department either."

Issue: Communication

"It's true, you can ask three different managers and get three different answers. It's frustrating; but then, we are not always consistent, either."

"If you ask Dad, you get one answer; if you ask Mom you get another. But then again, we don't always tell them the same story."

Issue: Conflict

"It's not only the supervisors who put us down and get angry at us. We can't seem to get along with each other, either."

"I can understand that the kids hate it when we yell at them and I don't like it when we yell at each other."

Issue: Respect

"The employees just don't function as a team. Those who have been here the longest don't care about the new people."

Issue: Empowerment

"They never ask for our input; on the other hand, we don't share at meetings when they do ask us for ideas."

"I wish the kids would see what needs to be done around here and do it, without being told; at the same time, when they do something without our asking, we don't usually express much appreciation."

If these kinds of statements come early in the process, it would be wise to allow some time to go by before making sure that many of the group members agree with the statement made.

Sometimes a group will be unable or unwilling to transition. This group will blame others continually, seeing no ownership for the issues. When a group is stuck in denial, care must be taken so that the meeting doesn't turn into a gripe session. Outside facilitators do so by being more directive than accepting and validating. Example of directive statements might be:

> "I've been hearing what management is doing. What about with each other–how is that going?"

> "You've outlined what the other department is doing wrong. What do you think you could do differently to help correct the situation?"

> "We can appreciate how others are contributing to the problems; what part do you own?"

Regardless of the transition, one should allow adequate time for venting and catharsis, normally at least one to two hours. People also must identify specific issues that are impeding growth, development and empowerment. If group members spend enough time verbalizing past hurts, gaining a sense of commonality, questioning the utility of the process and feeling validated in an accepting atmosphere, they will be better prepared to identify issues.

ISSUE IDENTIFICATION

At this point, the group needs to answer questions such as:

- What do you need more of, the same of and less of from each other?
- What do you need more of, the same of and less of from management/parent/children?
- What are the payoffs and risks for keeping things the same?
- What are the payoffs and risks for changing things?

When dealing with groups of management personnel, it may be helpful to add questions such as, "If we surveyed your employees, what would they say about your strengths and weaknesses?"

At work, to facilitate the issue identification process and make the exchange of ideas safer for all concerned, it makes sense to break the group into smaller subgroups. Each subgroup can assign a spokesperson to record and later report the group's answers to the previous questions. The information is processed when each spokesperson reports their team's answers to the questions. This may last 30 to 60 minutes, but letting people talk is healthy. It is helpful not to have supervisors present at this stage, since it may impede the free flow of communication–people may be reluctant to divulge information about flaws in the system or problems with a supervisor if that supervisor is present.

At home, to facilitate the issue identification process, parents should convene a family meeting. At this meeting, family members should be allowed to state what their issues are or identify what they want more of, the same of, or less of from parents and each other without others getting defensive or judgmental. One of the family members should write down what everyone says.

In this situation, parents should listen for transition statements, as noted previously. When these statements occur, progress can be made toward reaching an agreement amenable to all. Should the transition from blaming others to looking at oneself NOT occur, parents first will want to acknowledge the concerns raised by the children. Second, they can ask the children to review what role they play in the problem by saying something such as, "We understand your problems with Mother and me, but how do you kids feel that you may be contributing to those conflicts?" While the work groups report back what was said, the information is recorded on a flip chart for all to see. The flip chart papers are posted in a visible place for reference during future discussions. It should be noted that all information written on the flip chart should be typed and returned to the employees and the supervisors so that a baseline is established from which future progress can be compared. This helps to document what was said and establish action plans for both management and staff that will help everyone work cohesively towards correcting problems. In the family, each member should also have an opportunity to review the identified issues.

Later those same issues are revisited, and the participants are asked to identify which of the items they have control over and which they do not. In this manner, participants can deal with issues they have the ability to correct and without focusing on issues they cannot resolve. The value of this should be self-evident: It helps to direct the problem-solving efforts inward, thus avoiding victimization. It also allows problems to get solved rather than just talked about.

Everyone knows the Pareto Principle—the 80/20 rule: 80 percent of the work is done by 20 percent of the people, 80 percent of the problems are caused by 20 percent of the issues, etc. The principle applies here. If the participants tackle 20 percent of the issues they identified that they have control over, 80 percent of their problems will be taken care of. Then they can work a little at a time to deal with some of the others. They can use dispute resolution approaches or any other approaches afforded to them. But remember, before a group is willing to learn new techniques, the old baggage must be taken care of. Before you can be understood, you must first understand.

Sometimes, work groups and families feel confused about knowing how to most effectively deal with issues they've identified. Typical questions are:

- How can we change our attitudes and feelings when we've been this way so long?

- How can we communicate and confront each other without making things worse?

- How can we resolve our issues and move forward?

Answers to these questions and more will be covered in the first three steps of Harnessing the Power of Conflict:

STEP ONE:	Understanding Human Behavior
STEP TWO:	Using Leveling/Constructive Confrontation
STEP THREE:	Using Mediation as an Alternative Dispute Resolution

It should be noted here that the success of Harnessing the Power of Conflict is always enhanced dramatically if those in authority (supervisors and parents) who receive the information are receptive. When participants have been honest in identifying problem areas, authority figures sometimes have a difficult time accepting issues identified as weaknesses or areas they need to correct. It's easy for authority figures to be impressed with participants' promises to improve things among themselves. But it is more difficult to accept what participants say they need from those in authority. Most authority figures accept the information openly, albeit with some hurt feelings for a while. Most will create their own action plan to try to make improvements.

But whether issues are real or merely perceived as real, they need to be treated as valid. If they are not treated as such, participants cannot release them. While treating all issues as valid, we should still be able to identify those issues that need to be addressed from the issues that just need to be vented and heard.

Feelings are spared if people realize that positive characteristics have been raised, as well. There may be monumental problems, but good things happen even in the worst of situations. Even a stopped clock is right twice a day. In the worst family and work situations, where negatives have been identified, some positive statements help maintain balance. When the participants are asked what they want to see more of, the same of and less of, the "more of" and "same of" statements are usually the positive elements and the "less of" statements represent the negative elements.

However, we should all be forewarned that when the questions are asked, the answers will be given, so don't ask if you don't want to know. It is ludicrous to ask how someone feels and then get angry when they tell you. Keep in mind that while the issue identification process can be painful when negative issues are raised, it is better to look at them honestly than to ignore the feelings and perceptions of group members and have the issues continue to exist underground. Those concerned never have the opportunity to change or make things better in that type of situation. If authority figures try to reprimand participants for bringing up negative issues, participants obviously will feel betrayed. The loss of respect and the destruction of effective communication within the group may be irreparable.

CHAPTER FOUR

Key Points to Consider:

- People need a chance to voice concerns.

- Process is as important as outcome.

- Transition away from blame to ownership.

- Whether issues are real or perceived, they must at least be heard.

- Reactions of those in authority are important.

Harnessing The Power of Conflict

CHAPTER FIVE
Harnessing the Power of Conflict

UNDERSTANDING
HUMAN BEHAVIOR

THE PSYCHOLOGY OF BELIEF SYSTEMS/PERCEPTION

In any human interaction, it is helpful to have some way of understanding other people's behavior, thinking and feelings. Many of us make assumptions about why people behave the way they do, but few truly strive to understand. Moreover, without understanding we lack an effective communication strategy. In training executives and managers in how to deal with conflicted situations, we usually ask, "What's your strategy, methodology or game plan on how to approach and potentially deal with this type of situation?" Most look at us like deer in the headlights, stunned and frozen. For they realize that they do not have a well-crafted and theoretically sound approach. In fact, if they have an approach at all, it is eye for an eye.

Most of us employ an eye for an eye communication strategy, whereby tend to react to others as we think they are acting towards us. Gandhi once said, "An eye for an eye and everyone will go blind." We generally lack a conceptual framework to make sense of the people we deal with day in and day out. The typical result is that we become poor communicators.

Understanding human behavior and communicating effectively is not an easy task. Since the beginning of time, people have tried to explain human behavior. Greek and Roman philosophers debated the essence of man. When Sigmund Freud began documenting his work, the general population became interested in such issues as the conscious versus the unconscious and id, ego and super ego. Ever since Freud, there have arisen a number of schools of thought and theories of psychology. But applying a theory to work group interaction, conflict management and problem solving requires a theoretical framework that is functional and observable. A theory that makes sense in the family room, bedroom and the boardroom must also apply to those on the loading dock.

Shakespeare once said, "There's nothing either good or bad but thinking makes it so." Alfred Adler, a noted psychiatrist in the 1930s, applied that same principle to psychology, saying that a person's behavior springs from his ideas. He said that a person relates to the world based on his own interpretation of himself and his present problem and not by anything predetermined. He also noted that attitudes determine relationships to the outside world. Everything depends on opinion.

In the 1950s, Albert Ellis founded what he called Rational Emotive Therapy, or RET. Basing his thoughts on those of others before him and fueled by his growing dissatisfaction with traditional approaches to understanding human experiences, Ellis found that people's beliefs influenced their feelings and behaviors more so than events of the outside world (Corsini, 1973).

This theory applies to Harnessing the Power of Conflict, and the following components are the basic principles inherent in the process used here to show why others, as well as we ourselves, feel and behave the way we do. Moreover, all the techniques presented later in this book (confrontation, mediation, code of conduct, action planning and coaching) relate to this theoretical orientation. Stated simply, we must not focus on feelings, behaviors or positions but on the perceptions and needs that give rise to those feelings, behaviors and positions.

Most of us are familiar with the S ➡R model of human
S behavior.

In the presence of a certain stimulus, a specific response is elicited (show a dog meat and it will salivate). This theory
R has been applied to people and work groups (reward a job well done, and people will be proud and will work harder).

In our daily lives, most of us feel that the S ➡ R concept is true. How many times have we said things like:

"You're making me crazy."

"You make me angry when you do that."

"You make me feel worthless when you criticize me."

"Everyone wants to quit because you make it miserable around here."

"You don't do your share of the work, and it makes me sick."

"I can't stand being around you anymore."

These statements indicate that an outside event causes a feeling in a person, or one person's behavior causes a feeling or action in another. What Shakespeare, Adler and Ellis found is that this is not necessarily true. They discovered that something happens between the stimulus and the response that causes the feelings and reactions. If this were not true, then why can the same stimulus elicit different responses in different people? For example, a wage freeze may cause one to feel happy ("I'm glad I still have my job and there wasn't a layoff"), another to feel angry ("I'm not making enough now as it is"), another confusion ("What's a wage freeze?"), and still another indifference ("Who cares? What else can they do to us around here?").

In families when a child gets caught in a lie, some parents might yell ("This is just horrible"), others may be passive ("I'm sure she didn't mean to"), while others may lecture ("She needs a good talking-to"), or others may sit down and talk with the child ("We need to find out what's going on").

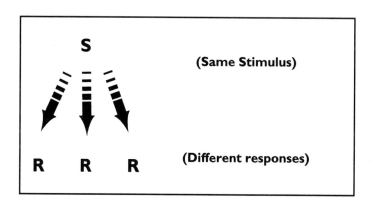

The model actually looks more like this:

What takes place in between the stimulus, or event, and the variety of responses, or feelings, is a third factor called the belief system, self-talk or perceptions.

It is helpful to view this in the framework of the Rational Emotive Therapy Model of Albert Ellis. Ellis looked at the stimulus as an activating event (labeled "A," Fig. 1), the belief system as perceptions or self talk (labeled "B") and the response as

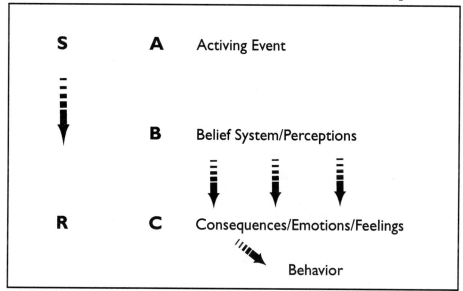

Figure I

the feelings or emotional consequences (labeled "C") (Corsini, 1973).

Following this theoretical framework, the perceptions (B) cause the emotions (C), not the activating event (A). Keep in mind that once we feel, the feelings drive our behavior.

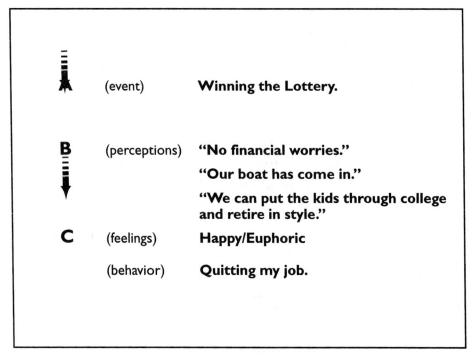

A	(event)	**Winning the Lottery.**
B	(perceptions)	**"No financial worries."**
		"Our boat has come in."
		"We can put the kids through college and retire in style."
C	(feelings)	**Happy/Euphoric**
	(behavior)	**Quitting my job.**

The following illustrates the concept, in sequence:

As you can see, it is not the event (A) that causes the happiness/ euphoria and the job resignation; it is the perceptions of financial security that cause the feelings of happiness, and those feelings drive the behavior (quitting).

At work, the same theory applies. For example: If your supervisor would walk into your office and say, "I need to see you in my office pronto!" and then abruptly would walk out of the office, how would you feel? Most of us would look at the events, perceptions and resulting feelings as follows:

A	(event)	**Boss's request.**
B	(perceptions)	**"What did I do wrong?"**
		"She's obviously not happy about something I said,"
		"I hope she doesn't rip me to shreds."
C	(feelings)	**Nervous, anxious, afraid.**
	(behavior)	**Avoidant/back peddling.**

Other possibilities are as follows:

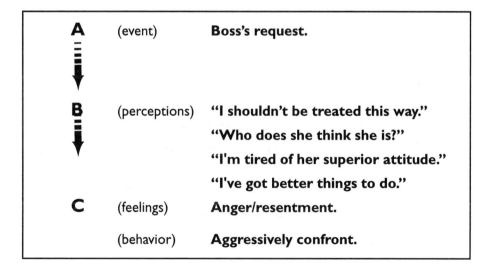

A	(event)	**Boss's request.**
B	(perceptions)	**"I shouldn't be treated this way."**
		"Who does she think she is?"
		"I'm tired of her superior attitude."
		"I've got better things to do."
C	(feelings)	**Anger/resentment.**
	(behavior)	**Aggressively confront.**

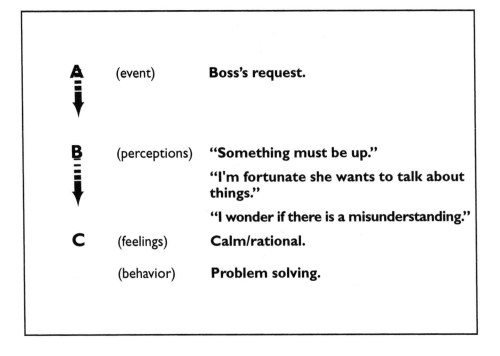

Was it the fact that the supervisor walked into your office that caused these feelings of anger, frustration or nervousness? The answer to that question is no. What caused the feelings is what you told yourself about why the supervisor was in your office.

The perceptions (B) drive the feelings (C) and the subsequent behavior. The events (A) do not cause the feelings. This explains why people can react differently to the same event or situation. Have you ever felt different emotions about the same event? In accepting a job promotion or transfer you might feel excited, yet slightly scared or apprehensive. Why? Because you are telling yourself that it is a compliment to be promoted or transferred, but it is new and unknown.

The same principles apply at home as well. Let's look at the child's lie again and see how it would appear:

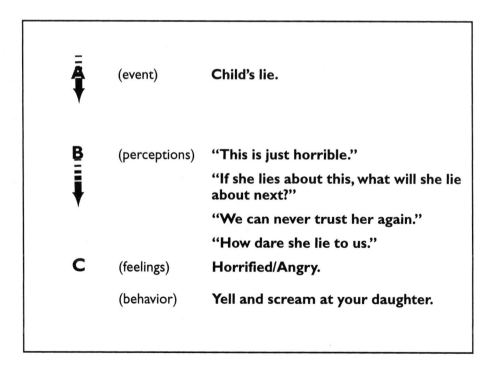

A	(event)	**Child's lie.**
B	(perceptions)	**"This is just horrible."**
		"If she lies about this, what will she lie about next?"
		"We can never trust her again."
		"How dare she lie to us."
C	(feelings)	**Horrified/Angry.**
	(behavior)	**Yell and scream at your daughter.**

Other possibilities may be:

A (event)	Child's lie.
↓		
B (perceptions)	"Well, we're going to put a stop to this right now!"
		"Just who does she think she is?"
↓	"We haven't raised a liar."
		"She certainly needs to be set straight."
C (feelings)	Indignant/Betrayed.
(behavior)	Lecturing/Talking down or to her.

Yet another possibility:

A (event)	Child's lie.
↓		
B (perceptions)	"This is not like her to lie."
		"She needs to know, whatever happened, we will be easier on her if she makes a mistake and tells the truth than try to lie and cover it up."
↓	"We need to find out why she made such a poor choice."
		"She certainly needs to be set straight."
C (feelings)	Disappointment/Frustration.
(behavior)	Problem solving/talking with your child.

Our belief systems/perceptions/self-talk drive our behavior. If I believe that I am getting put down by a sarcastic comment from you, even if you didn't intend it to be so, I may feel angry; and my resulting behavior might be either a verbal attack, ignoring you or walking out of a meeting. The belief system/perception/self-talk caused my behavior. If you didn't understand my belief system at that point, you may be totally shocked by my behavior.

So it is clear we need to look at our own perceptions, as well as those of others, to understand why we all feel and behave the way we do. Perception is the engine that drives the train. Feelings and subsequent behavior are the caboose. They are side effects or by-products of our perceptions. If you had pneumonia and were coughing, I could give you cough syrup and you would cough less. But the disease or pathology would be left untreated. We need to deal with perceptions and not feelings if we want to change behaviors. This is not to say that feelings are not important. Although feelings should be acknowledged, it is in the perceptions where a person has the greatest chance of influencing behavior.

Where do perceptions come from? Perceptions are made up of values, morals, past learning, traumatic events, other life events, parental messages, current events and our life experiences. They are the lenses through which we see the world. Sometimes the lenses are distorted. If they are, we see the world in a distorted fashion. Everything is filtered through the belief system, perceptions or what we tell ourselves (self-talk). This is how we evaluate the in our lives. If our lenses (perceptions/self-talk) are skewed even 10 degrees right or left of center (reality), then our feelings and behavior will be equally skewed 10 degrees right or left of center (reality). And if the perceptions are grossly inaccurate, the resulting feelings and behaviors will be grossly inaccurate, as well. While there are many ways we can see reality in a distorted fashion, there seem to be four primary critical perception errors that can negatively impact our feelings, behaviors and our interactions with others.

PERCEPTION ERROR #1: POLARIZATION

The first of these errors is called polarization. This is the tendency to view reality in polar opposites (sometimes referred to as "either-or thinking"). Some examples of the polarized thinking include:

Good	⇒ Bad
Victim	⇒ Empowered
Generous	⇒ Selfish
Up	⇒ Down
Right	⇒ Wrong
For us	⇒ Against us
Elated	⇒ Depressed
Productive	⇒ Useless
Together	⇒ Separate
Wonderful	⇒ Horrible

The list can go on.

We learn these polarities early on in life. If you weren't a good little boy or girl, what was the only other option? Probably bad or naughty. Rarely did your parents come home and say, "My, you are so mediocre today!" If you attempted something new, you either succeeded or failed.

In adulthood, the same polarizations are still evident in most of us. We have a good boss or a bad boss, we have a good day or a bad day, or a good evaluation or a bad evaluation. When our belief systems are locked into wrong or right, good or bad, yes or no, then our feelings and behavior will follow accordingly.

If we see events in the polarities, our feelings and behavior will swing wildly as a result. A person who has extreme mood swings is on an emotional roller coaster; way up one minute and down the next. Again, this is a result of perception polarization, not changing events. If you work with or have a relationship with someone who is on an emotional roller coaster, you get to go on the ride for free.

In reality, events are usually shades of grey. They are matters of degree, and few of them are absolute. If we can shift our thinking and see life as a continuum rather than as a series of polar opposites, we can experience many more emotional and behavioral options-options that are more reflective of reality.

> ⇒ Good
> ⇒ Pretty good
> ⇒ O.K
> ⇒ Adequate
> ⇒ Par
> ⇒ Sub-par
> ⇒ Disappointing
> ⇒ Irritating
> ⇒ Not good
> ⇒Bad

We are doomed to polarities unless we choose to alter our perceptions and see the world for what it is. This is not to say that we need to look at everything as wonderful–the "power of positive thinking" idea. We are not suggesting that you think of yourself as a flower waiting to bloom or see each day as a growth experience. We call that the art of positively lying to yourself. It reminds us of the old advertisement about, "Is the half a glass of water half full or half empty?" We don't know about you, but to us, it's just half a glass of water (reality). You can dress it up and say, "The glass is half full", or dress it down and respond, "The water is half gone." If you have ever been through a downsizing or rightsizing, you could say," You know what? We have twice as much glass as we need!" The point is that we need to view things as they are. If we do, we can avoid escalating a mildly frustrating event into a nuclear disaster, thus expending more much anger and energy than is warranted. This is not to say that bad or awful events don't just happen; they do. But we challenge you to wonder if they happen with the regularity that we see them.

PERCEPTION ERROR #2: AWFULIZING

This brings us to the second critical error: awfulizing, or the skewing of emotions that labeling causes. When we "awfulize" to extremes, then our feelings and behaviors again will follow. Have you ever said to yourself, "This is the worst possible thing that could have happened to me. It's horrible!" Or "Why did this happen to me. What did I do to deserve this?" If we talk to ourselves like this, labeling events as awful, horrible, terrible or catastrophic, how do we expect to feel? Perky? It isn't going to happen. You are going to feel awful, horrible, terrible and catastrophic and will behave accordingly. And you will be miserable to be around.

What do you want on your tombstone? Crabby? Intense? A pain in the butt? The one at work who always tried to shoot down new ideas? Unless you come back as a bird or a rock, you only get one shot at life. And if you whiff, there's no do-over. This is no dress rehearsal. We see so many people who get up in the morning already feeling overwhelmed and under-appreciated. They get themselves to the office and have a to-do list for the day that could not be accomplished in a week. They get home and see that the house is a mess, feeling no one else at home helps out. The dog threw up. They cook dinner, pay the bills, go to bed and wake up–only to do it all over again.

Again, the beliefs or perceptions cause the feelings and resulting behaviors. To avoid awfulizing, we need to watch the words or labels we use to evaluate our life events. We need to ask ourselves, "Is this really bad, awful or horrible?" Some events are. If so, go ahead and feel terrible. But terrible events rarely happen weekly, daily or hourly, unless we choose to see them that way. Ask yourself, "Is it awful, or is it merely a pain? Is it just disappointing or irritating? A nuclear war that destroys society is the worst possible catastrophe–everything else is an inconvenience.

Where does this tendency to awfulize come from? As a child, if you got four A's and one D on your report card, what did you spend dinner talking about? We seem to be oriented toward the negative in order to fix it but seem to shy away from what's going well and celebrating.

We had a coaching client who saw his accomplishments as, "at least I didn't screw it up" or as "dodging bullets." When he perceived himself in this manner, he would feel relief or moderate anxiety, but would never really feel good, excited or satisfied. When he was able to accurately see his accomplishments for the successes and triumphs they were, then and only then could he feel successful or triumphant. Many counseling clients that suffer from depression will admit to awfulizing or at least minimizing events in their lives in an effort to not feel too good, assuming that the better they feel, the more likely a negative event will occur ("Just when I start to feel better something always comes along to knock me back down"). If they were feeling too good, they would really crash hard when the next bad thing happened. Not true. Simply stated, if we perceive badly, if we label awfully, we will feel poorly. The alternative is to believe in the continuum, which drives behaviors in a much more real way and which gives us more choices.

PERCEPTION ERROR #3: SELF-DEPRECIATION

The third critical error is self-depreciation. If our self-esteem was measured like oil in our cars, many of us would be a quart or two low (some people wouldn't register on the dipstick.) This low self-esteem can be turned inward. This type of self-talk sounds like:

"How can I be so stupid?" or

"I really am a screw-up," or

"What did I ever do to deserve this?"

If my self-esteem is low, I may feel responsible for how others feel and behave. If someone is upset, I may turn on myself and wonder what I did to cause that feeling in them ("It must have been me"). Or I might say, "Let me apologize now for the mistakes I will make in the future." But really you're not so powerful that you can cause others to feel and behave in ways they don't choose. Turning on ourselves leaves us few options for change and lots of opportunities for victimization, and the resulting inaction, depression, unassertive behavior and non-participation. If we think we are inadequate and terrible and a failure again, the feelings and behaviors surely will show it.

Sometimes self-depreciation can show itself in the downplaying of accomplishments. Some people can't seem to take a compliment. We hear, "Oh it was nothing" or "It's no big deal really; anybody could've done it". With just a couple of self-defeating perceptions, they totally negate the reality of the compliment, don't feel special and fade into the woodwork.

The opposite reaction to this way of thinking also can be toxic when we blame and project our low self-esteem or problems on everyone else rather than owning some of the responsibility ourselves. The resulting feelings will be hostility, aggressiveness and grandiosity.

"The V.P. is cheating us again... The supervisor is out to get me... They don't realize how valuable I am to this company."

These are the people who chronically feel like they get the short end of the stick. Nothing is good enough, fast enough or fair enough. If you said, "My it's a nice day," they would respond, "Yeah, if it doesn't rain." If they won $1 million in the lottery, they'd say something like, "It's a rip-off. You don't really win a million dollars. You only get $750,000. The state takes $250,000 for taxes. They're a bunch of liars. Why don't they just call it the $750,000 lottery and be honest about it? If I had known that, I would'nt have spent a buck on the lousy ticket." These people can be very unpleasant to be around.

PERCEPTION ERROR #4 OVERGENERALIZATION

Ellis, in his landmark publication, "Guide to Rational Living," (now in its third printing, 1997, Wilshire Book Co.) and Dr. Burns, author of "Feeling Good" (1997, Avon Books), both describe a perception error of overgeneralization. This occurs when we use such labels as *always, never, can't, have to, ought to, must and should.*

Always, never and *can't* represent a negative experience in the past that is generalized as a never-ending pattern now and projected into the future. Perceptions such as, "I *always* seem to screw things up," "I *never* get what I really want" or "I *can't* seem to do anything right" are just not true. At some point in life, today in fact, you have accomplished something without making a mistake (arrived at the office without crashing your car, for example). Day in and day out most of us get our needs met (nourishment, socialization, shelter). And every day we do things right (tie our shoes, make a phone call, get to where we are going). Granted, everyone makes mistakes: We settle for something less than what we want, and we have times where things don't go as planned. But is it really an ongoing, never-ending life pattern? If you think this way, you will feel defeated, anxious and unmotivated.

Have to, ought to, must and *should* are labels we use in an attempt to motivate ourselves-for example, "I *have* to do well," "I *must* succeed," "I *should* do more." These statements produce unnecessary pressure and resentment. Ellis once called this *musturbation,* and self-help groups refer to this as *"shoulding"* on yourself. When we label events in this fashion, we become apathetic, unmotivated and set up for failure. Moreover, when we apply labels to others, such as, "He shouldn't treat me like that" or "I have to be treated with respect," we become so resentful that others can't reach our level of expectations.

These examples show the problems associated with perception errors and illustrate how much our own self-talk drives our feelings and behaviors. The good news is that we have a lot more control over these things than we think we do. We may have little control over the activating events (A), but we have plenty of control over the perceptions (B) and thus can influence our feelings (C) and our resulting actions. If we can listen to where others are coming from, we can influence the feelings and resulting actions from them, as well, through constructive confrontation and mediation.

The theoretical concept presented here has use not only in understanding others but ourselves, as well. Rather than looking at events, behaviors or situations, we need to focus on perceptions and belief systems in order to understand others and ourselves. Although we may have little or no control over events, we do have control over our beliefs and perceptions. We can choose how to view them.

If we want to change how we feel or behave, we need to change how we perceive events and situations. Since we cannot control our co workers or family members, we can at least control how we respond to them. We can examine how we are viewing situations to see if they are accurate.

Most people will say they are aware of the events that occur in their lives, as well as their feelings and behavior: but they're not sure if they are really aware of their perceptions or self-talk.

An event can occur, and we immediately feel something and respond quickly. Like when you're talking to your 15-year-old daughter, and in the middle of the conversation, she rolls her eyes and says, "Whatever!!" you probably get instantly crazy and say or do something you wish you hadn't. That is the power of association. Over time we learn, in a healthy or unhealthy way, to respond to certain events in a predetermined manner. But somewhere along the line, thoughts (self-talk) or perceptions must occur. We all have our buttons; when they're pushed, we respond.

To find out what our own perceptions or self-talk are, we need to talk them out or write them down. Get them out of our heads and expose them to reality. Thoughts in our heads are like an endless loop that just goes around and around like a dog chasing its tail or a run-on sentence. But when perceptions are spoken or written, they become straight and linear. Then and only then can we evaluate them to see if they reflect reality.

Have you ever been in an argument with someone and realized that what you are saying is wrong, but you keep on arguing anyway? Or have you ever been reprimanding your child and realize you sound just like your own mother or father (and you swore to yourself you would never sound that way)? It's because you got your thoughts out of your head and you **heard** them for the first time. This is why it is important to talk with a friend, spouse, counselor or co-worker, to get the perceptions out so they can be evaluated. Another idea is to keep a journal or diary so you can see your perceptions. We suggest writing something simple, like the following:

A. **Event** (What happened?)

B. **Perceptions** (What am I thinking or saying to myself about the event?)

C. **Feelings** (What am I feeling?)

Over time, patterns of perceptions will emerge, indicating if any of the critical thinking errors are present or some other form of distortion is occurring. Once we identify how we are perceiving events, we can choose to change them to better reflect reality or conclude that they do reflect reality and proceed.

Hopefully this gives an insight into self and others and perhaps explains feelings and behavior. For ourselves, if we see that our perceptions are distorted, we can change them and thus change how we feel and behave. Again, it is not the power of positive thinking. We are not saying that a person should perceive bad things as good, as if a nuclear bomb dropping really is a mere inconvenience. What we are saying is that we can get along with others better when we see that everything isn't awful and catastrophic and that everything is not worth 100 percent of our energy. If we see the world as it is—not in black or white but in shades of grey—we won't overreact. If we understand perceptions as a way of trying to understand feelings and behavior, we'll have a much stronger foundation for better communication and problem solving.

This theory of human behavior is the foundation for the rest of the book in developing skills to make us better communicators and problem solvers. As you can see, feelings and behavior are side effects of perceptions. They are by-products of our thoughts. Since we have the most control over our perceptions—not events, feelings or behaviors—we need to focus on perceptions to be effective communicators and problem solvers.

Feelings and behaviors are clues to you as you interact with others. If someone is way up and down emotionally, you can predict that they are polarizing. If someone seems to be angry and irritable, they might be awfulizing. Likewise, if someone seems apathetic, unmotivated or avoidant, they could be self-depreciating or over-generalizing. You need to listen for and verbally challenge those distorted perceptions to help them see the event more realistically.

CHAPTER FIVE

Key Points to Consider:

- Perceptions, not events cause feelings.

- Avoid the four critical thinking errors: polarizing, awfulizing, self-depreciation and over-generalizing.

- If you alter perceptions, behaviors and feelings will also change.

- Feelings and behavior are clues to others' perceptions.

- Distored perceptions need to be challenged in order to change.

Harnessing The Power of Conflict

CHAPTER SIX

COMMUNICATION AND CONSTRUCTIVE CONFRONTATION

The step involving effective communication and constructive confrontation is known as the Leveling Process.

There is no escaping conflict or confrontation, no matter if you are in the boardroom, bedroom or family room. At times it seems that we just float from one conflicted situation to another. Whether this is because of our contemporary, fast-paced lifestyles or global warming is not known. What we do know is that most of us AVOID conflict and confrontation or save up conflicts like green stamps and cash them in when we have a full book, generally ripping the other person to shreds and feeling guilty ourselves.

Most of our inability to handle conflict originates from our past experiences in handling difficult situations or people. How many confrontations did you win with your parents while growing up? What would have been the likely response if you said to your mother or father, "Mom, Dad, I've polled my brothers and sisters and we have a list of 10 demands on how you need to change"? You probably would not have heard, "Yes dear, you're right; we do need to change." You may have heard something more like, "Just who do you think you are to talk to me that way? Go to your room!" How many confrontations did you win with teachers, traffic cops, customer relations, people or supervisors? If we're honest, we have to admit most of us have a negative perception or belief when it comes to dealing successfully with conflict.

The good news is that there is plenty we can do to confront people effectively and manage conflict. All it takes is applying some common sense and adhering to a few basic principles. Here are those principles:

1. To effectively and assertively express yourself, you first need to own your feelings and behavior. Eleanor Roosevelt once said, "No one can make you feel inferior without your permission." No one or no event can cause you to feel or behave in any way that you do not choose. We cannot control events and other people, but we can control how we feel and our reactions and take ownership of them.

If we do not accept responsibility, we likely will communicate in "You" messages. We'll say such things as, "You make me so angry," "You are driving me crazy" or "You make me feel so worthless." These are blaming statements to which most people do not respond in a positive fashion. These kinds of statements won't elicit a group hug or an invitation to dinner.

If we do accept responsibility for feelings, we'll make statements more like, "I feel angry when you don't communicate with me, because then I think the relationship is one-sided" or "I feel worthless when you talk to me that way, because it puts me down." This is an assertive way to communicate how you feel and how you see things. It is not insubordinate or necessarily antagonistic. While some spouses, peers, co-workers, bosses and children may respond with something like, "I'm sorry, that's not what I meant" or "I didn't mean to hurt your feelings," other people may get defensive. This leads to the second principle.

2. Most problems can be solved by simply listening and truly trying to understand the other person. But most of us don't do that. We are so driven to get our point across or to defend or explain ourselves, we get lost in our own heads. Our objective is to understand the other person, whether we are being confronted or whether we are confronting someone else.

If your 8-year-old said, "You don't care about me. You spend all your time working or cleaning the house," you could respond in a number of ways, such as, "Well, sometimes I don't feel like you care about me either" (fighting back) or "Mommy has been very busy" (rationalizing) or "Oh, come on now, you know I spend as much time with you as I can" (minimizing) or "I'm doing the best I can" (defending).

Instead, next time listen and respond with a statement that indicates that you do understand–for example, "It sounds like you're feeling left out" or "It seems that you think I'm not spending enough time with you."

Now keep in mind there is a big difference between understanding and agreeing with someone. You may feel that you are spending all the possible waking moments you have with the child, but getting that point across to the child is not important initially. What's important is that your 8-year-old feels heard and that you understand the child's feelings. Then, and only then, can you solve problems and generate options. Perhaps just hearing the child's concerns will be enough.

The same principle applies if you're doing the confronting. Let's say you need to tell the boss that your work is stymied when she doesn't get back to you with decisions in a timely fashion. You may say, "Ms. Fishbeck, I need to tell you I feel stymied when you don't get back to me, because then I am unsure how to proceed." She may respond with, "I get back to you as fast as possible. I have other priorities around here, you know" or "You know, you might need to be a little more independent rather than always relying on me."

At this point you will need to fight the natural tendencies to use the F word...to say "FINE" and walk away. Also, fight the urge to get defensive or over-explain your position. Here again, just like with your 8-year-old, you need to communicate your understanding, not necessarily your agreement. Responses such as "I am sure you have multiple priorities and are very busy" or "You're feeling that I lean on you too much for direction?" indicate that you understand and are willing to listen. Even if you reflect back the wrong feeling or sentiment, the other person simply will correct you. If, for example, your partner said "I wish our sex life was more spontaneous and daring," and you responded, "So you think I'm dull in bed?" but this was not what your partner intended, he or she will correct your interpretation. It would sound something like, "No, all I'm saying is we need to spice things up a bit" or "I'm not feeling that you are dull, it's just that things seem to be getting a little routine."

In our training seminars, some participants make an accusation that this process is "techniquing" or parroting people. It is not. Techniquing people occurs when you reflect back everything a person says or you reflect only the content of what was being said, and not the feelings. If a co-worker were to call you a weasel, you wouldn't ask, "So, you think I'm a small burrowing mammal?" Responding to the feeling with, "It seems as though you feel angry with me" is much more appropriate. Likewise, if the boss was discussing her vacation in the Bahamas and said, "Man, my trip to the Bahamas was great!" a techniquing response would sound like the following:

"You went to the Bahamas and it was great?"

(Boss) "Yeah, we spent all our time at the beach."

"You spent all your time at the beach?"

(Boss) "Well, not all our time. We visited some of the shops."

"You went shopping too?"

(Boss) "Oh just forget it. What's wrong with you?"

"You want me to forget this conversation and are concerned about me?"

If you did this, people would think you truly have gone over the edge. One of many possible responses that would not be techniquing or parroting the boss could be, "Your vacation sounds like it was just what you needed."

Now that the person feels understood, you can:

a. Get back to the point of the confrontation.

b. Stop the discussion if listening was sufficient.

c. Try problem-solving, if necessary.

3. Regardless, the third principle must be considered: Whatever communication strategy you use needs to nurture or enhance the relationship and not damage it. If you are not listening, but instead are trying to get your two cents in first, win the argument or become aggressive, you can expect that it will damage the relationship. If you think in terms of winners and losers, everyone loses. What good does it do us if I win and you lose when we still need to live or work together?

However, if the relationship has no value to you, go ahead and do whatever you want. Let's say you're in a remote city that you'll probably never visit again. You go through the drive-up window at a fast food restaurant and get shorted your cheeseburger. In a remote city, you could ask, "Do you remember birth?" while you pull the kid's head through the little window. However, in your hometown, this would not be advisable, because you may want to eat there again–or you may know the kid's family.

The same logic applies to business or family relations. Our primary objective is to enhance relationships–getting away from winners and losers–because we have ongoing relationships with those in our businesses and families. This approach addresses the problem instead of attacking the person. Once the relationship is secure, then and only then will you be able to communicate your point of view and/or problem-solve.

In order for you to be heard after you have attempted to understand the other person, an empathy statement can be very useful. Going back to your 8-year-old, you could say, "I can understand that at times you feel like I don't care about you because I'm busy; but I do love you and want to spend as much time as possible with you. I just wish there were more hours in the day to fit everything in." With the boss, an empathy statement might sound something like, "I can appreciate that you have a full plate. All I'm saying is that the quicker I get a response from you, the more efficient I can be" or "Perhaps I could be more independent; I just want to do the best job possible without trying to assume I know what you need." Even if you disagree with the other person's opinion, first show that you understand, and then give your point of view. Remember, it's the quality of the relationship that is important.

There are no magic formulas in handling conflict or touchy situations. All too often our emotions get in the way and we wind up creating a bigger problem. Stephen Covey once said, "Common sense is not common practice," and it definitely applies here. Hopefully, you can find some common sense in accepting your feelings and behavior and can work on understanding before you are understood to enhance your relationships.

CONFLICT OPTIONS

There are a variety of conflict resolution options: You have the mediation/problem-solving option. But you can also preserve the relationship at the expense of making the point (pacifying); negotiate; escape (and neither make the point nor preserve the relationship); or make the other person do it (at the expense of the relationship). There are times when any of these styles may be appropriate.

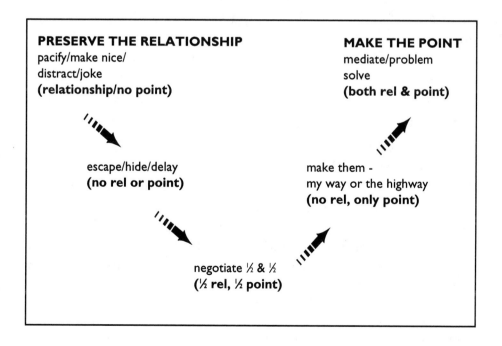

PRESERVE THE RELATIONSHIP
pacify/make nice/
distract/joke
(relationship/no point)

MAKE THE POINT
mediate/problem
solve
(both rel & point)

escape/hide/delay
(no rel or point)

make them -
my way or the highway
(no rel, only point)

negotiate ½ & ½
(½ rel, ½ point)

COMMUNICATION AND CONFRONTATION

We don't always learn the proper ways to communicate assertively. Regrettably, there wasn't a class on this in grade school. The word "confrontation" conjures up fear with most people, probably because most of us didn't exactly win most of our confrontations in our developmental years. In addition, we probably haven't won many later in life. So our track record isn't good. And even if we learned how to confront, it still seems uncomfortable because of our negative experiences.

Here is the first opportunity to use the art of changing perceptions, self-talk or belief systems. Here is the opportunity to view confrontation as a relationship-building and nurturing experience.

What do we mean by that? Doesn't confrontation usually lead to anything but relationship building or nurturing? *Actually, the opposite is true.* If we never express our feelings–and subsequently our perceptions–to others, they never will have an opportunity to explain their actions, apologize, defend their position with us or problem-solve with us. We never will have the opportunity to work it all out. And if we never tell someone that what they are doing is hurting us, themselves or others, we are guilty of passive approval–that is, we condone the behavior and enable it.

For example, let's say someone at work is making disparaging remarks about a co-worker you like. You say nothing. The person making the remarks likely will believe you agree–and, in fact, has every right to believe you agree. So the person making the remarks continues to make them, which hurts the co-worker. By confronting the situation, many people's feelings may have been spared. The offender may have learned a valuable lesson about gossip and may think twice before speaking about someone in an improper way next time.

Confrontation is essential to preserving an ongoing relationship. It is not the yelling at each other or arguing that we may have experienced as a child. It is problem-solving at its best. If the relationship is to be preserved, confrontation at some point will be necessary. It may not be necessary to work at a relationship that is NOT ongoing. But if we want to nurture an ongoing relationship, we will need to talk it through, or confront at some point. When we engage in actions that hurt the relationship, we may find it will not be ongoing for long.

Actions that hurt the relationship include angry outbursts (when you can't take it any longer), keeping silent and keeping it all inside (pretending everything is OK when it isn't) or yelling–just to name a few. Confrontation does not include any of these things. Confrontation is not yelling. It is communicating assertively, expressing needs and listening to the needs of others in order to problem-solve.

There is obviously a right and a wrong way to confront someone. You can say, "You have a face that will stop a clock" or you can say, "When I look at you, time stands still." In either case you get your message across, but the first way may get you in more trouble than the second. Although confrontation takes us out of our comfort zones, the process that follows should make it easier.

Years ago, Thomas Gordon recognized the effectiveness of confrontation in his work with children. In his book on parent effectiveness training, Gordon stated that people who have problems with children can either change themselves or the child, among other options.

Let us assume that you wish to modify the behavior of another person, or at least how that person interacts with you. Before you start, be sure you understand the problem. Be clear on what your issue is and pick the mountain you want to die on. That is, confront on only the issues that are most important to you. Take a stand on the hill that is worth defending. You wouldn't want to waste a confrontation on a minor issue; doing so may further deteriorate a relationship because the person may feel that you are making mountains out of molehills.

When economic inflation occurs, our dollar becomes worth less. Print too many dollars, and they diminish in value. In a like manner, initiate too many confrontations, and they too diminish in value. Be clear on which important issue you wish to discuss.

Begin the conversation with an "I" message. Do not begin with flattery or small talk ("My, what a lovely tie" or "Isn't it cloudy today?") These messages dilute the impact of what you are saying. "I" messages usually can be worded as follows:

I think _____.

I need _____.

I feel _____**when you** _____

because _____.

Examples would sound like:

"I think we should save money for our vacation."

"I need the toys picked up from the driveway now."

"I feel angry when you don't pitch in, because then I have to do more than my share of the work."

Contrast this with typical "You" messages–accusing statements that use the word You:

"You always spend our money right before we need it for our trip."

"You brats pick up those toys now before I really get mad!"

"If you would get up off your duff and help me, maybe I'd get out of work on time for a change. Don't be so lazy!"

We guarantee that if you use You messages, the people you are confronting will not jump to their feet to apologize and do what you ask with smiles on their faces.

When "I" messages are used, the focus is placed on how a person's behavior impacts you. Make sure you deal with what is happening, and do not attack or use labels. Labels (lazy, shiftless, bad attitude, careless) hurt too much to help and are likely to trigger more anger and defensiveness. Be careful not to send a hidden attack disguised as an "I" message:

"When little brats don't pick up their toys, I get angry and need them picked up."

"If certain people would quit being so lazy, I wouldn't have to work so hard. I need cooperation."

As you can see, there is a subtle slam sandwiched in between these "I" statements. It still will evoke a negative response from the recipient, who more than likely will hear only the attack and not the "I" statement.

After receiving an "I" message, the recipient will still be defensive and may elect to justify, rationalize, blame, defend, withdraw, use humor or minimize so as not to have to own the defensive feelings. We all sting when receiving negative feedback, no matter how constructive the intention. So if we don't like receiving criticism we can imagine that others don't either. Expect defensiveness; then, if it doesn't occur, you can be pleasantly surprised.

A person either may get quiet, accept the feedback or attack back. In any case, it is important to acknowledge the feeling and "pull it through," so to speak, to get to the person's perceptions. It is a temptation at this point to play in the feelings area and get angry and defensive when someone else is being defensive with us. If we let that happen, we may find ourselves in a heated argument instead of a problem-solving confrontation. In order not to play into the feelings–to get to the perceptions which you can influence–you must "ju jitsu" through the feelings; that is, acknowledge the feelings and pull them through. As Fisher states, unlike street fighting (where force is met with force), ju jitsu is a martial art in which force is met with a step to one side and the pulling-through of the opponent, using his own force to knock him down (Fisher, 1988).

Often we can ju jitsu a person's feelings out of the way in order to get to their perceptions by merely using "You" messages. "You" messages are listening statements, and can be of three types: passive listening, active listening and empathetic listening.

Passive listening occurs when nothing is said, and "uh-huh" typically is given as the most verbose response. The sole purpose of passive listening is to let the other person continue to vent or speak. It lets them go on without your interruption or comment. It draws quiet people out and helps them to feel comfortable enough to continue.

Active listening is useful only when clarification of content is desired. If we are unsure of what the other person is saying, we can reflect back what we heard to more fully understand their thinking.

(You think_____.)

Empathetic listening is the most useful method, where the feelings of the other person are reflected back in order to get to the perceptions.

(You feel_____.)

Sometimes people don't even know what they are saying, because the message is mixed in with such intense feelings. When you acknowledge a feeling with a You message, you do three things:

1. You clarify the feeling.

2. You keep yourself from reacting and thus starting a war.

3. You show the other person that you heard the feeling, which calms the person down and allows you to get into the area of perceptions so that you can problem-solve. Ninety-nine percent

of the time, a simple "You" message will catapult a person right to their perceptions. And once we are dealing with perceptions, we can influence behavior easier. An example would be:

("I" message) "I'm sick and tired of having so much work to do and having no help."

("I" message response) "Aw, don't be such a martyr. You sit on your duff once in a while just like the rest of us, so don't go getting uppity with me about how you do all the work."

("You" message) "So you feel that I'm nit-picking, and that you are doing your share of the work?"

("You" message response) "Yeah–we all work hard, and I'm ticked when I get accused of being lazy."

("You" message) "You think I'm attacking you and saying you're lazy?"

("You" message response) "Well, maybe you don't mean it that way, but that's sure how it sounds."

Notice how the tone begins to get less hostile after a couple of You messages. It settles things. It also keeps the person who is confronting from getting angry and arguing back to defend herself. If the "You" messages weren't used, the exchange may have sounded more like this:

("I" message) "I get sick and tired of doing all the work around here and getting no help."

("I" message response) "Aw, quit being such a martyr. We all sit on our duffs once in a while; and besides, I get sick and tired of you getting on your high horse and attacking us."

(No "You" message used) "Me? What about you? You can't even work for the whole shift! And how dare you accuse me of sitting on MY duff..."

"Aw, get away from me, there's no talking to you ...you're not the boss."

"If I were the boss, I'd fire a lazy lout like you."

"Oh yeah? Wanna take it outside?"

This time, the problem escalated into a possible physical confrontation.

Even reflecting back the wrong message is OK. Remember, "You" messages also give us an opportunity to clarify. If we get the message wrong, the other person will just correct us. For example, if someone said,

"Boy, some of us are really in a foul mood today."

And you said,

"So you're not having a good day?"

The other person would probably say,

"No! I'm referring to you. You seem to be the one in the bad mood."

Empathetic listening seems to be more effective at diffusing anger than active listening. Here again we can see that responding to the feeling is more powerful than to the content.

When attempting to use "You" messages effectively, we must resist the temptation of the NEGATIVE ALTERNATIVES of *ordering, warning, preaching, advising, criticizing or teaching* (Gordon, 1975). Let's say your spouse comes home from work and says, "I can't stand that place anymore. I'd like to quit." An example of an effective You message might be:

"You feel angry about work." (feeling)

Your spouse will likely respond, "Yeah, the boss criticized my report again." (perception)

Notice how the spouse goes right from feelings to perceptions. Now you can discuss things, problem-solve or merely listen–whatever seems called for. If you were to use the negative alternatives, your responses may have been ineffective and may have sounded like this:

(order) "You better not quit. We need the money."

(warn) "If you do, you may not get a job like that again."

(preach) "I felt like that at my job. I just told the boss where to get off, and she backed off after that. I think a person like that boss needs to get a lesson on self-control."

(advise) "Why don't you just tell the boss to go pound sand?"

(criticize) "Can't you handle that jerk yet? You've been there for four years, and we go through this every other night."

(teach) "Practice it with me: I'll be the boss, and you tell me where to get off."

Sometimes we might even interrogate, which we think is actively listening. But this can be frustrating and may escalate the other person's anger. ("What did the boss say? Did you tell her where to get off? Does she pick on all the people or just you? How is Myrna handling it?") Remember, the objective is to listen and not respond yet. "You" messages can be used after you confront someone if they get defensive, or you can use them to help you keep control if you are being confronted by someone else. For example, if you were at your desk and someone came in and said:

"You never answer your messages, and I really needed to talk to you. That makes me mad."

You could respond:

"You are angry because you needed to get a hold of me and I didn't return your call."

After sending "I" messages and "You" messages, and after the person has calmed down and has told you what his perceptions are, then it is time to restate your position and express your needs. Normally, this begins with an empathy statement, such as:

I can appreciate how you'd feel_____.

I can understand how you could think that_____.

Hey, I'd feel that way too if I thought that_____, followed by:

But all I'm saying is that I need_____.

The person either will move into discussion with you, or you can just listen. If the person is still angry, you can continue to use You messages and empathy statements until she is calm enough to continue or until you deem it necessary to end the conversation. Even if it isn't all settled when you end the conversation, at least the person will have heard you, and you can leave without carrying the anger or stress of unfinished business.

A complete exchange might go something like this (your dialogue will be in bold):

"I'm sick of you not doing your share of the work. We've all been talking and everyone thinks you need to work harder."

(You message) "What you're saying is that I've been sloughing off."

"Yeah ... we all worked an extra weekend, and you didn't volunteer. That honks us off."

(Empathy statement) "And I can appreciate how that would look to all of you. If I thought someone was getting away with murder, I'd be honked off too."

"We aren't saying you did it intentionally, but we'd like it to be fair."

(Empathy statement) "I can appreciate how you want things to be equitable. So do I. All I want is to have a schedule that is fair, but one where we get some notice in advance. My weekend was scheduled, and we were going to be out of town. What you all don't know is that I told the boss I'd do two weekends next month since I didn't do any this month."

"We didn't know that, but I'm sure everyone will understand now. Look, let's just drop it."

"Don't feel bad about bringing it up to me. I'm glad you did. I would rather talk about it than to have people talking behind my back."

Remember that the purpose of this method is to open channels of communication, but a more important purpose is to PRESERVE THE RELATIONSHIP. What's the use of winning the battle if you lose the war? Confrontation such as this can actually nurture the relationship, as it did in the example above. Both parties now have a better understanding of each other's behavior and have been honest and open in the process.

Sometimes it's not what you say but how you say it. If my 17-year-old wants a new car and we can't afford one, I can say,

"Don't talk to me about the car; I don't want to hear about it."

Or I can say,

"I can understand that you feel like your old car isn't very nice, and I'd like to be able to get one for you; but I'm afraid we'll have to wait a while."

Who would you rather talk to next time you have a problem? I'd go to the person who listened to me. It is important to understand that I need to hear you before you will have any desire to hear me.

What has been talked about can be summarized as follows:

THE LEVELING PROCESS
(Constructive Confrontation)

1. I need_____.

2. You feel_____.

3. I can appreciate how you'd feel_____, and I'd probably feel that way too if I thought_____; but all I'm saying is that I need_____.

What do you do when dealing with someone who has authority or power over you?   When people have positional power over you, it means that they have power, a title or line authority that you don't have. You probably cannot force them to do what you want them to do. You may have only limited impact. The power you may have lies in persuasion. Again, if you influence perceptions, you can focus on how to make things better and preserve the relationship. Remember: If someone attacks, let the person vent and then jump in. Bring him up to your level, but do not descend to his; that is, don't play his game. If you fight back, you take the focus off of the issues. Pick the mountain you want to die on, as we said before. When is it worth fighting, and when is it better to give in? Here are some suggestions on how to deal with positionally powerful people who are adversarial:

1. Try to deal with their thinking errors, if they have them.

Are they polarizing, awfulizing or reflecting low self-esteem via being hyper agreeable or hyper-aggressive? (If so, gently challenge their thinking by providing options or different ways of looking at the problem.) For example, a doctor says to a nurse manager, "The staff nurses are talking against me; they are insubordinate. One of them challenged what I was doing with Mrs. Jones in 402."

The nurse manager, sensing polarizing, says, "That could be true, doctor. But could it also that the nurse, who sees himself as part of the treatment team, gave you the suggestion not in a spirit of insubordination, but because he felt comfortable talking to you?"

The doctor may or may not buy the explanation, but it will give her something to think about.

Another example could be that an employee hears his supervisor say, " We have the worst sales figures ever! I sure hope that people realize their lack of effort may cause layoffs here." (awfulizing)

The employee says, "Well, Sandy, lack of effort may be the reason, but it could also be the economy. I would hate to see people laid off before we see how other sales teams are doing, in case it is the economy."

In both cases, the person acknowledges that the superior's explanation statement COULD be true, but then provides an alternative way of thinking. When people hear the critical thinking errors, a gentle challenge to them may help get them out of the extremes and back to center again.

2. Try leveling.

Sometimes the leveling process may be a great way of dealing with those above us. Be careful that there is no insubordinate tone used. An example might be that a boss is getting ready to replace a person who has not been given an adequate chance. The person about to be fired might say,

"Bill, I can understand your frustration with me. Maybe I haven't always showed you what you wanted to see; despite that, I wonder if I can get a little more time to get some training or coaching and then try again. (Step one of the leveling process: Talking about an implied need–in this case, "I need a second chance." This shows that you don't have to use the process verbatim, especially if different words are more comfortable for you.)

The boss says, "I've given you more chances than I normally give others, Ted. I think it's better to separate and give you a chance to succeed somewhere else."

The employee replies, "So you feel that the situation with me is beyond repair?"

The boss replies, "It seems that way."

The employee says, "Maybe it is, Bill. But with the costs of recruitment and orientation, I sure would appreciate you letting me have one more stab at this."

If the answer is no, at least the employee did everything possible to try to convince the boss that he deserves another chance.

3. If leveling doesn't work, comment on what happened.

An employee tells the superior after a discussion gone bad, "I thought this discussion would help us work better together; but I can see that this isn't working out. Let's try again."

OR, if there is no chance of convincing the person in the future, the employee might say, "I'm sorry you feel that way," and then leave. Remember: Sometimes escaping is the best choice.

4. Speaking of escaping, one option also could include the use of one of the other conflict styles, such as pacifying, negotiating or forcing.

Forcing may be a difficult choice with a superior; but if the person is morally or ethically wrong, it may have to be used. *Pacifying* can be used when emotions are running rampant with the superior. *Withdrawal* can be used when there is a stalemate and the person cannot hope to win, or when continuing could mean loss of the job or damage to the relationship. (It doesn't make sense to win at the expense of the ongoing relationship.)

Negotiating is used when you have to give something up to get what you need. (You want the weekend off, so you are willing to work later during the week because you are in the middle of a big project.)

5. Remember not to set up winners and losers, or else you both lose—especially when you're dealing with those in authority.

Avoid putting the superior in a spot by giving an ultimatum. ("Do this my way, or I'm out of here.") Take this approach, and you may not like the choice that person makes.

6. If the boss won't support you and none of the options work, it's OK to let go and vent to trusted parties and then think, "Can I impact it? Am I looking at things correctly, and can I manage the stress that it is causing me?" Then decide if you can live with it or if you must leave.

7. If attacked, you can always say, "You may have a point there. Let me get back to you on that."

This gives you time to get out of the hostile situation and think of what you want to do or say. It also disengages the person. If you don't verbally punch back, there is no fight.

8. Look for something in common.

"It sounds like you don't like being dumped on, and I have to tell you, neither do I. Let's look for a way to get this done without either of us being dumped on."

9. Look for opportunities to uplift the other person.

Sometimes, this has shock value and positive outcomes occur. Find something the person did or said that was good or correct, and point it out in a note or email later on. ("I thought about what you said, Bob, and you are right ... we need to get more focused here. Thanks for taking the time to share that with me. I think it will help me get some things done on time.") Instead of starting another battle, compliment the person on something he said or did, and you may be surprised at how positively he responds to you. Positive breeds positive, and negative breeds negative.

10. Do the opposite of what you think you should do.

The character George on the popular sitcom *Seinfeld* did this once. Since his thinking always seemed to get him in trouble, George did the opposite of what he thought he should do. You can do the same thing, by:

a. Not fighting back, but backing down.

b. Not tattling, but keeping your mouth shut.

c. Not arguing but complimenting. (Don't be phony ... give the person a compliment they EARNED.)

What if you're not sure what to say?

There are many books on the subject of emotional intelligence. One of them, by Dr. Weisinger, a licensed psychologist and leading authority on this subject, states that understanding yourself, managing your emotions and then effectively communicating are important in getting the right message across at the appropriate time. In his book, *Emotional Intelligence at Work* (San Francisco, Josey Bass, 1998), Dr. Weisinger lists tips on how to make accurate appraisals so that we don't make misinterpretations based on too little information. He suggests that we don't overgeneralize, use destructive labels, make assumptions (mind-read), have strict paradigms on how others should act, or give too much significance to events (Weisinger, 32-34). This will help in making more accurate assessments of people and how to appropriately respond to them. Timing also is important. Sometimes withdrawal lets us have time to evaluate what to say and how to respond.

What other factors influence how the message is received from others when leveling with them?

Tone of voice, facial expressions, eye contact and gestures are all nonverbal factors that may influence how a message is received by someone. I can say things in many different ways using different tones of voice, and the same message will be picked up differently. Think of the word "wonderful." Use it to describe the best vacation you have ever had. Now use the word to describe how you feel about your least favorite relative coming from out of town to stay at your house for a week to freeload. Now use it with your child to describe her getting a "D" on her report card. As you can see, one word can carry different meanings by how you say it.

When a junior high school child who is supposedly doing homework is found in his room with school clothes all over the floor, eating pizza one hour before dinner with the TV blaring while talking on a cell phone to a friend, and you say, "Clean up and get ready for dinner, which you better eat," and the child screams, "FINE, I'm COMING!" is it his words that make you angry, or his tone of voice and facial expression? Facial expression can be of critical importance in communicating with another. In his book, *The Tipping Point* (New York, Little-Brown, 2000), Malcolm Gladwell studies how little things make a difference on big things. When one candidate was being discussed on a news broadcast, the anchor gave a subtle smile. Apparently, that subtle cue was picked up, because more people who watched that broadcast and that anchor voted for that candidate. Because people don't filter out biases when they watch the news, they may be affected by these signals without even knowing about them. Nonverbal cues are as important as verbal; as Gladwell puts it, "The subtle circumstances surrounding how we say things may matter more than what we say" (Gladwell, 1979). We need to keep a check on how we communicate to people. Am I making eye contact? If I am not, am I sending a message that this person is not important? Am I frowning when they are speaking or smiling and nodding affirmatively? Does my tone of voice or facial expression send another meaning than my message? Be careful of how you level with another. Watch the word choice. Avoid the barbed-wire words we speak of in the Helpful Tips Chapter (Chapter 12). Labels can be barbed-wire words. We think we are communicating quickly, which may be true; but in effect, we are hurting someone, who may, in turn, become defensive. So words like, "You are uncooperative" or "You are insubordinate" may do more harm than good.

What are some examples of successful leveling?

Let's look at some opening statements in different circumstances that may help you begin the leveling process.

To describe poor work performance to an employee:

"Mary, I've noticed that you haven't been meeting the performance standards. I need to have all team members meet at least the minimum standards."

To talk to a supervisor who reprimanded you in front of your peers:

"Bob, I've been thinking about the verbal reprimand the other day, and I felt embarrassed that others heard it. I wish that could have been done in private."

To talk to a child about a bad report card grade:

"Sue, I had hoped you'd pass all the subjects in school. I want to talk to you about how you can improve your math grade next quarter."

To talk to a parent about an undeserved punishment:

"Mom, I know you are angry at me for not coming home before curfew, but I feel two weeks grounding, including not being able to go to Homecoming, is harsh."

Practice framing the opening sentences in implied or stated "I need" messages. Depending on the reaction, the conversation can go in many directions, but remember:

- Know your hot-buttons so you don't lose control. If you feel out of control, just say, "I'm getting angry, so I'd rather talk when we can both be calm."

- The relationship is of the utmost importance. Don't sacrifice the relationship to make a point.

- Use "I need" or "I feel___when you____" messages as openers, either stating those words or implying them.

- Watch the barbed-wire words. Watch the tone of voice and facial expressions, like laughing or smiling, when someone is leveling with you or when you are communicating something serious.

- Use "you feel____" to show an understanding of another's feelings.

- Use empathy statements, such as "I can appreciate how you'd feel____", when you understand someone's perceptions.

Finally, know that a failed attempt at leveling does not mean the process didn't work or that you screwed up. The attempt helps to preserve the relationship. Just trying the process will help show people you are making an attempt at understanding them. It will pay off.

STAY OR GO...OR, WHEN IS "ENOUGH ENOUGH?"

In dealing with others or evaluating anything, it is important–if not imperative–to have a mental strategy or structure. How do we approach a problem or situation? How do we know that we are evaluating it accurately? How can we best manage it if it's unresolvable? When is enough enough, and when do we need to get out or remove ourselves from the situation?

Whether we are evaluating a job or a relationship, we need to do it in a systematic fashion so that if we elect to get out, we can do so with the confidence that we have tried everything else humanly possible. We want to avoid regret down the road from making a hasty or emotional decision. We want to avoid saying to ourselves, "If only I would have, could have or should have." As a rule of thumb, most problematic situations or relationships can be approached by asking the following three questions:

1. Can I impact the event?

2. Am I perceiving it or looking at it accurately?

3. Can I manage the stress associated with it?

The first question asks if you can impact the event, meaning, **"What can you do to change the event?"** If the event is a problem with a co-worker, supervisor, significant other or child, we need to ask ourselves, "What can I do (not what do they need to do) to change the event or problem?" If the problem is with a co-worker or supervisor, you could confront her, try to understand her perception, problem-solve, ask for help in resolving the problem or go to Human Resources or the next level of management. If the problematic event is with a family member or a significant relationship, you could try to talk about it, go for counseling, yell and scream about it, try to ignore it or pull rank. Again, you need to ask yourself if you can go directly to the event to try to influence it and make it better. If you can, it may or may not work out for the better, but it may be better than complaining about it to all who will listen. Nor do you want to avoid dealing with it directly (enabling) or aggravate the event.

If you have tried to directly affect the event and the desired effect didn't occur, then you must ask yourself this question: "Do I stay or do I go?" Most of us at this point will elect to stay. If you do so, then the second step comes into play–asking yourself, **"Am I looking at this situation accurately? How important is it? Can I let it go?"**

You need to examine your perceptions of the problematic event. Are you viewing it correctly? Are you guilty of viewing the event with one of the critical thinking errors mentioned earlier (polarizing, awfulizing or breeding low self-esteem)? Separating out the events from perceptions and feelings is helpful when you're trying to identify your perception or view. Talking with a friend or professional (or reading about the problem) will help to give you a different perspective on the problem. If you are perceiving the event incorrectly, your perceptions can be changed to be more reflective of reality.

Sometimes, you need to ask yourself, "Just how important is it?" About seven out of 10 times, if you ask yourself that question and answer it honestly, you'll realize that the problem isn't that important. If it truly is important, then you need to deal with it. If your 15-year-old daughter gets decent grades, her hair is roughly one color, she is involved in school activities and doesn't do drugs or alcohol, but her room is a disaster area, how much do you really want to argue about it? While it would be better if she were tidy, basically she is a pretty good child; so maybe the messy room isn't that important after all.

In one of our consultations, we met two people on the supervisory level (we'll call them Mary and Sue) who worked in an agency that provided services to a four-county region. Mary had a habit of asking Sue's staff to help her without first consulting Sue. Sue would become enraged, but would keep it all in, only to explode later. Sue's perception was that Mary did this because she didn't respect her and felt that this behavior undermined her authority. They were supposed to be equals.

Sue requested a meeting with the director. Mary stated that she didn't mean any disrespect but that when she was short of help and Sue wasn't around, she didn't have time to find Sue. She felt that Sue was overly sensitive about this and needed to let it go.

Since Sue wanted to check out her perceptions, she wrote them down and consulted with a trusted colleague to see if he shared her perceptions. Since the mind is an endless loop, if you just think about things to yourself, you will detour all over the place. Talking it over or writing it out makes it clearer. Sue did this, and thus entertained different ways of viewing the behavior of Mary: "Maybe she is just trying to get the job done. My people still respect me, so maybe my authority isn't undermined."

After checking out perceptions, Sue changed them. When perceptions are accurate, you are faced with the decision again–do I stay or do I go? As Sue did in this instance, most people at this point elect to stay. If the perceptions are accurate and you cannot impact the event, then you must proceed to the next step, which asks, **"Can I manage the stress?"** (Besides, if you have developed the habit of eating and making mortgage payments, you may need to stay.)

If you elect to stay, there is a wealth of stress management information available today. The important thing is for people to actually USE something and not just make resolutions. Getting active and shifting the focus away from the event may help.

Sometimes, no matter what you do or try, it isn't enough to handle the stress. In this case, you are forced to make the last stay-or-go decision. At this point, many elect to go, or are asked to go, but will do so feeling like a failure with a sense of defeat.

However, if you elect to go, it could be the healthiest choice for you. If you have tried to impact the event, evaluated your perceptions, and attempted to manage the stress to no avail, then maybe going is the most positive thing to do. The alternative may be to become bitter and unpleasant, which is toxic to yourself and those around you.

CHAPTER SIX

Key Points to Consider:

- Use Confrontation Process. ("I" message, "You" message, empathy statements)

- Confrontation nurtures relationships.

- You must first understand in order to be understood.

- When is enough enough?

Harnessing The Power of Conflict

CHAPTER SEVEN
Leading, Learning and Living

DISPUTE RESOLUTION PROCESS

Alternative Dispute Resolution

As we have seen, there are many ways to solve conflicts. We can pacify others, telling them what they want to hear, or gloss over the issues. We can escape by choosing not to deal with conflicts. We can make others do what we want by using the force of authority-"because I said so." We can negotiate, in which everyone gives up something to get part of what they wanted.

Using problem-solving techniques is another alternative in dealing with conflict. But it is the one alternative we have the least productive experience with. When problem-solving, we start by simply listening and acknowledging the other person's feelings or thoughts. We can use the leveling process or constructive confrontation to make our points while attempting to preserve the relationship. But about half the time, this alone is not sufficient to really resolve the conflict.

When conflict persists, most of us look outside of ourselves for someone to make the decision for us or to represent our position to some higher authority. This higher authority could be a court of law, supervisor, grievance committee, parent, friend, union steward, spouse, consultant or arbitrator. Some groups may simply take a vote.

In our seminars, we remind people to be careful what they ask for, because they just might get it! Do you really want someone to decide for you?

If someone decides for us, it may turn into a big win or a big lose proposition. We may or may not get what we want. If the relationship with the other party is ongoing, we risk winning-but by winning, we damage the relationship. If we win at the expense of the relationship, our win/lose proposition quickly becomes lose/lose. While this may be necessary at times, this approach is more of a last resort. Before getting to that last resort, many companies and individuals are turning to an alternative dispute resolution process known as **mediation**.

Mediation has evolved with many interesting applications and has been gaining in popularity throughout the U.S. and internationally, as well. Mediation is defined as the intervention of a neutral third party in a dispute in an attempt to reconcile differences, usually at the request of all parties.

Mediation is not necessarily a new concept. The roots of mediation can be traced back to international disputes in the 19th century-between Greece and Turkey in 1868-69, between Bolivia and Chile in 1882, and Germany and Spain in 1885. Mediation was advocated and promoted at the Hague conferences of 1885 and 1907. Later the League of Nations provided for mediation of disputes culminating in the United Nations procedures for obligatory mediation for member nations. Closer to home the United States formed the Federal Mediation and Conciliation Service in 1947. This agency offers mediation services in handling disputes between labor and management or may enter into the negotiation process when interstate commerce is affected.

Today, mediation is available to help resolve all kinds of disputes:

- divorce and custody disputes
- labor and management
- employer/employee relations
- sexual harassment
- workers comp.
- co-worker
- partnerships
- family members
- landlord/tenant
- insurance claims
- victims and offenders
- neighbor disputes
- consumer disputes
- business disputes

Benefits of mediation include:

- empowerment
- win/win mutual agreement
- cost effectiveness
- confidentiality
- privacy in dealing with a confidential cost effect method of problem resolution
- orientation toward future
- enhanced relationships
- informal atmosphere
- participatory process

As you can see, the applications and benefits of mediation are getting broader. Take for example divorce and custody mediation. In days gone by, divorcing couples would hire two attorneys and battle in court over such issues as who would get what possessions, who would get custody of the children and when would each parent be with the children. Frequently, divorcing couples would not speak to each other directly, but only through their attorneys. The conventional wisdom was that two people mired in this type of conflict could not possibly come together to make rational decisions about their children's future. Someone had to do it for them. (A poor assumption, and a costly one!) Typically, one parent would win big and the other lose big. And in the final analysis, every family member came out a loser.

Nothing is further from the truth than to think two people can't handle their own conflict. In fact, national statistics indicate that in divorce and custody mediation, mutual agreements are reached with divorcing couples 60 percent to 70 percent of the time. Now, some will say that is a low number. But considering that a few years ago the percentage was zero, it is a major achievement. In some states, judges have the ability to mandate (court order) divorcing couples to a minimum number of hours in mediation. More and more, however, couples are electing to use mediation on a voluntary basis as an alternative to the traditional judicial process. Research indicates that mediated agreements have a lower incidence of later winding up in court as opposed to judge-decreed agreements. Also, ongoing relationships, as fragile as they may be, are better preserved, laying a positive foundation for future problem-solving and conflict resolution.

So, if divorcing couples or warring nations can settle their differences, what is it about these mediation techniques that can help a company struggling with downsizing, diversity, growth, quality improvement or change? In a word, the answer is plenty. Mediation gives us a structure to challenge old paradigms, involve those affected by the outcomes, create ownership of problems and solutions, and promote win/win agreements in an nonadversarial, partnership atmosphere.

With Harnessing the Power of Conflict, we have enjoyed a mutually beneficial agreement rate of 75 percent to 80 percent. Work groups agreeing on how to interact differently will improve the quality of their working relationships, whether they are two-person partnerships or Fortune 500 companies.

The rest of this chapter focuses on the techniques inherent to the mediation process. These techniques can be applied as a whole process. Or they can be used in segments that will be helpful in your day-to-day interactions with others as you go about transforming your work or family relationships. In a company, the result will be good working relationships that promote quality services and products. In a family, the result can be healthy family interactions, regardless of the family structure.

THE CUSTOMARY APPROACH: THREE-STEP PROBLEM SOLVING

The best way to illustrate the basic principles of mediation is to contrast them with the way most groups, companies and families approach problem solving. As you read through, please note the difference between positional and needs-based problem solving. The customary three-step problem solving approach is also called positional bargaining or positional problem solving. It can be diagrammed as follows:

1. Identify issues or problems.

2. Formulate positions or solutions.

3. Discuss.

STEP #1: IDENTIFY ISSUES OR PROBLEMS

While this step is essentially the same in both problem-solving methods, a common mistake is to spend too little time concretely identifying all the issues. If the issues are ill-defined, there likely will be little agreement that the issues identified are the major ones, and it won't make any difference what solutions are developed. If a physician misdiagnoses a patient's condition, it won't matter what new drug or high-tech treatment is prescribed; it won't treat the pathology.   So it's always important that the issues be operationally defined and the participants be able to buy into them.

STEP #2: POSITIONS/SOLUTIONS

Once the issues are identified, or sometimes even before the issues are identified, we usually start formulating positions. Perhaps, we even start to muster support among our peers and others for our positions, like picking sides on the playground. We begin politicking to see who is for us or against us. We may start calling in our markers, favors owed us from others.

In a fast-paced, ever-changing environment, once a problem surfaces, people immediately start asking the question, "What are we going to do about it?" This is when factionalism or sub-grouping occurs. Now that all parties have formulated their positions, the next step is to convene some type of forum to select the best position.

STEP #3: DISCUSSION

Now a meeting is held to discuss the different positions. In reality, what happens is that we simply argue over who has the better position. Each side is trying to win, consciously or unconsciously, at the expense of the other. This is the methodology most of us grew up with.

No one is listening to understand the other side's position, but only listening for ways to counter. This funnel-down technique is commonly used, and it commonly results in an either/or proposition that promotes winners and losers. When one side wins, it damages the quality of the ongoing relationships.

Rarely does the position with the best merit win. The winner is the side which makes the most persuasive argument. Often no agreement is reached, and all parties suffer the consequences (hurt feelings, resentment, strained relationships, lower-quality products or services ... sometimes even war).

This positional method is how families solve problems most of the time. Let's take, for example, the husband and wife trying to decide what to do on Friday night (the issue). The wife declares that she would like to go out for dinner, and the husband counters with his desire to go to the movies (their positions). Having committed to their positions early in the problem-solving process, they decide to sit down and talk about it (the discussion). The ensuing discussion usually sounds something like this:

Husband: "I want to go to a movie."

Wife: "I want to go out for dinner."

Husband: "Well, hon, we could eat popcorn at the theater. They have that new popcorn oil that's non-caloric."

Wife: "That's ridiculous. Besides, I just want to spend some time with you."

Husband: "We could get two seats right next to each other."

Wife: "You're not listening to me. We can never seem to talk."

Husband: "We have 15 minutes to kill to and from the theater. We can chat our fool heads off."

Wife: (angry and frustrated) "Fine! We'll just go to the lousy movie. We always do what you want to anyway." or "Just forget it. It isn't worth all this. I don't want to do anything now. I'm staying home."

Husband: (angry and frustrated) "We do not do everything I want to do. Just last week we went to your sister's when I didn't want to. Sometimes you can be such a martyr!" or "Fine! We'll just stay home then."

Oh boy, sounds like another fun time on Friday night, doesn't it? In some relationships, this is all too typical. Each spouse commits too early in the problem-solving process to a position. While the wife tries to give reasons why they should go out for dinner, the husband counters her reasons to fit his position. The wife begins to get frustrated and starts blaming, and the husband gets defensive and lashes back.

Another example: Let's say the boss, Ms. Fields, is having a discussion with one of her employees, Mr. Jones. She feels that expenses can be reduced best by eliminating positions. Mr. Jones wants to try to forestall that by cutting equipment and expenses first:

Ms. Fields: "Did you consider my cost savings proposal, Mr. Jones?"

Mr. Jones: "Yes, and I was wondering if we could take a look at different alternatives to layoffs."

Ms. Fields: "These aren't layoffs, they're position eliminations!"

Mr. Jones: "Fine, but can't we hold off on ordering the new equipment until sales catch up?"

Ms. Fields: "That won't work. We need the equipment to produce the products to make sales."

Mr. Jones: "What's the use if we don't have anyone to operate the equipment?"

Ms. Fields: "This isn't the time to be difficult, Mr. Jones. The expenses are on the salary side, not the supply or equipment side. I can't believe you don't see that. Maybe you're too soft. Know this: If we don't cut salaries, we'll close our doors!"

Mr. Jones: "I guess there's no choice then." (thinking, "Why did she ask me if she already had her mind made up?")

In this customary three-step approach to problem-solving, we formulate positions. In the mediation alternative approach, we formulate needs instead of positions. This is referred to as needs-based bargaining or needs-based problem-solving. It can be diagrammed as follows:

1. Identify issue/problem

2. Discuss

- Needs

- Shared interests

- Objective criteria

3. Position/solution

STEP #1: IDENTIFY ISSUES OR PROBLEMS

As in the customary three-step positional problem solving approach, all the issues in conflict need to be identified and operationally defined with buy-in from all parties. This is where reflective listening in an invaluable tool to generate comments such as, "Sounds like we all need more communication internally to be on the cutting edge." or "Seems most of us think that all the yelling and screaming is not getting us anywhere."

It doesn't make any sense to argue over whether or not something is an issue. If one party in an ongoing relationship perceives something as an important issue, it is.

Once the issues are defined and some type of consensus is reached, it's time to move on to the second step. Herein lies the difference in the two approaches.

STEP #2: DISCUSSION

In the mediation approach, you simply invert steps 2 and 3, where the discussion occurs before positions are formulated and the politicking begins. The discussion focuses on needs, shared interests and objective criteria rather than positions or solutions (Fisher & Ury, 1991).

Rather than asking, "What should we do?" a needs-based problem solver asks, "What does everyone need?" (needs). While needs may vary, they can often be categorized into the basic needs that most people, organizations or corporations have in common: trust, communication, honesty and respect.

Rather than initially focusing on our differences, let's focus on things we have in common (shared interests). In divorce and custody mediation, the mediator will focus on the love and concern parents share for their children, how both are important to the children's growth and development in spite of their differences. At work, we can use mediation techniques with a peer by starting with the interests we share. For example, we both want an equitable work load, to get off work on time, to have cooperative and collaborative relationships, to have a nonhostile work environment and respect for diversity. Initially, we can sharpen our shared interests, not our differences.

Agreeing on objective criteria is another part of mediation. If necessary, we can look to some measurement, benchmark or expert to help in the process (objective criteria). Using the Blue Book value is helpful in buying a used car. In divorce or custody mediation, sometimes counselors are called in for their opinions on what would be appropriate, given a child's age or maturity. Or accountants may be asked to render an opinion on equitable division of assets. In business, consultants are asked to make recommendations on specific problems.

STEP #3: POSITIONS/SOLUTIONS

At this point, the group needs to consider the expressed needs, shared interests or objective criteria from previous discussions to begin generating solutions or positions to meet everyone's needs and the shared interests. The question becomes, "What can we agree on that satisfies our needs and shared interests?" More times than not positions and solutions will emerge that no one thought of at the beginning. This is the creative funneling-up process at work. Here we are expanding the pie rather than dividing it (Ury, 1991).

Committing to a position too early in the problem-solving process blocks creativity and doesn't take into account the other party's needs and shared interests. Why just have two solutions (yours and theirs) when numerous solutions can be developed that meet specific needs? More importantly, a win/win agreement can be reached to meet the needs of all concerned while preserving relationships.

Back to the husband and wife. Had their problem-solving discussion been needs-based, it would have sounded like this:

Wife: "Tonight I need to get out of the house and just relax a little, away from the kids."

Husband: "I don't want to get all dressed up or be around a lot of people. I've been teaching all day and want to relax too."

Wife: "I don't want to be around a bunch of people, either. But I am getting a little hungry."

Husband: "Well, I'm not that hungry. Besides, if I eat one more burger or pizza this week, I'll explode."

Wife: "Maybe we could just go for a drive or go to the park for awhile."

Husband: "A drive sounds good. It gets us out of the house without bumping into a lot of people and if we decide later to get something to eat, there are plenty of fast food restaurants on the west side of town."

This sounds just a little different than the positional problem-solving approach and it produces a different outcome. Here the husband and wife first discuss needs and look for shared interests rather than staking out a position. Subsequently once the identified positions or solutions are developed (positions that neither thought of initially) they find the solution meets their mutual needs. This solution never would have been generated by the customary, positional method, because the spouses were locked into their respective positions of dinner or a movie.

Revisiting our cost-cutting scenario from the mediation (needs-based) approach may sound like this:

Ms. Fields: "I need to make sure we reduce expenses, and the salary budget is where we need to look."

Mr. Jones: "I need to work with you on expense reduction too, but I'd like to do so without putting our people out of work."

Ms. Fields: "Maybe we can talk to them and get them to agree to a wage freeze instead of job elimination."

Mr. Jones: "Maybe we can have enough people leaving through early retirement or by not filling open positions that costs are saved without laying off."

Ms. Fields: "Work up the numbers, and let's see what we have."

Again, once the needs were generated, positions emerged (wage freeze, early retirement, vacant positions left open) that no one thought of at the beginning.

The mediation approach can be used in interpersonal relationships at home and at work. It also can be the problem-solving approach of choice in more formal settings. As mentioned earlier, mediation is used as an alternative dispute resolution process for countries, businesses or legal disputes in which the parties involved desire a participatory and confidential process rather than a win/lose public process.

Mediation in more formal settings usually consists of five components or phases:

Phase I–Considerations

Phase II–Setting the stage

Phase III–Identifying issues

Phase IV–Reframing issues

Phase V–Getting agreement

Whether you are a participant in formal mediation, acting in the capacity of a mediator or simply are a parent or supervisor trying to find different ways to handle disputes, understanding the five essential components will be most helpful.

PHASE I:
CONSIDERATIONS

The first *consideration* is to determine whether mediation is an appropriate approach to use at all. In some instances it is not. In the following situations, mediation is not indicated:

- Do the parties involved have the power or authority to carry out any agreements reached in mediation? If employees from two different departments reach agreement on how to work more efficiently, will the boss back it up? If the kids decide how to split up the chores, will Mom and Dad go along? Do the diplomats have the authority from their respective countries to enter into agreements? If not, those parties that are empowered need to be involved to avoid a frustrating experience.

- If there is a question of impairment–that is, drug or alcohol abuse–mediation is not the process of choice. We certainly would not mediate an employee's or family member's alcohol or drug usage. Nor would it be appropriate to mediate if one of the parties involved in the mediation is himself impaired.

• If there is a tremendous imbalance of power, in which one party is a threat to the other, mediation should not be used. Do the employees fear retribution from their boss if they recommend changes? Do any of the parties feel fearful being in the same room with another party? A level playing field is necessary for agreements to be long lasting.

Secondly, we need to make sure that all the parties potentially affected are identified, willing to participate and are supportive of any agreements reached. At work, if the production and maintenance departments are going to mediate down-time issues, does engineering need to be involved? If we make corporate policy changes in the home office in New York, do we need to determine their impact on the branch office in Des Moines?

In 1996, the United States ignored this step when it passed the Helms Burton Law, which allows the U.S. to sue foreign countries that do business with Cuba. The U.S. failed to bring the international community into the process or to accurately gauge the impact of the U.S. acting unilaterally. Not only were the members of the World Trade Organization unsupportive, the European Union drew up legislation that would allow for foreign companies sued under Helms-Burton to countersue and collect damages.

Thirdly, we need to consider whether or not to caucus. That is, we need to determine whether a mediator should see the parties individually (in caucus) or together as a group. Caucusing is sometimes used in the beginning of mediation to allow the individual parties to vent feelings (if the emotional level is high), to assess each party's willingness to mediate, to identify issues and solicit buy-in into the mediation process. We can use caucusing at any time during mediation if emotions seem to be ruling over reason or an impasse develops. It also can be used if one party appears to have shut down and doesn't seem to be able to continue on a level playing field.

Whether Harnessing the Power of Conflict is used to mediate work group disputes or within a company that wants to identify issues and improve communication, caucusing is a good way to start. This facilitates transitioning–individuals and groups begin to quit blaming others as they look at how they themselves contribute to the problems. They're able to separate out what they can control and what they don't, focusing on what they can control and thus impact.

Even when caucusing, however, the parties do need to be brought together as soon as possible. Each party needs to hear the concerns of the other in a forum that allows each to tell their story. We have seen that when each party is allowed to speak, when each truly tries to listen, many misperceptions are exposed and cleared up. This cannot happen if caucusing is overused.

If Mom or Dad wants to use the mediation process for problem solving in the family, caucusing with each family member might not necessarily be a good idea, because it sets the parent apart from the process. Remember, we need a level playing field where all family members feel empowered so all parties feel that their thoughts and feelings are important. While parents retain veto power, they also can be a part of the problem, process and ultimate solutions. There are few more moving or rewarding experiences in life than to see parents and children listening to each other, owning their problems and inventing options that meet the family's needs.

Another consideration in this initial phase is whether to mediate with a second mediator, commonly referred to as co-mediation. Co-mediation is beneficial when a mediator is new to the process, when the parties are volatile or the issues are complex. In addition, mediators are human, and they may find themselves getting angry and frustrated at times. When this happens in co-mediation, the other mediator can take the lead. In teaching mediation in business, we find that in our role playing, participants soon discover that mediation is hard work and emotionally draining. Co-mediation allows the mediators to share the work.

Last, diversity needs to be considered. Luckily more work groups are striving to be more sensitive to this issue. It is important, because people from different cultures look at problem solving differently: Some are very formal, others informal; some have religion intertwined in the process, and others look for a separation of church and state; some cultures are autocratic, and others democratic; some are traditional, and others less so; some are more private, and others are not concerned with privacy.

When we mediated a Polish couple's court-ordered custody and co-parenting agreement, cultural issues became very apparent. Present for the initial mediation session were the mediator, the couple and two interpreters. After setting the stage and addressing the issues of custody, co-parenting schedules and primary residence, the ensuing discussion of "needs" promptly bogged down. We asked one of the interpreters, a Catholic priest, "What happened? Things had been going so well." The priest responded, "Polish people are very private, and they are embarrassed to talk about this in front of all of us. Now that the important issues are on the table, they want to talk between themselves and tell you what they can agree on and what they can't." In the next session, the couple reported to us what agreements they had reached and which ones they wanted the judge to decide.

PHASE II: SETTING THE STAGE/ESTABLISHING GROUND RULES

When starting mediation, it is important to define and discuss what is going to happen, how it is going to happen and what the likely outcomes might be. This second phase of mediation is called *setting the stage* or *establishing ground rules*. It helps orient the parties to the process and sets expectations for behavior while establishing the credibility of the mediator(s).

Explanation of the mediation process: Here the mediator explains that the mediation process is different from what the parties may be accustomed to. In mediation, we are not seeking to identify who is right or wrong, but are instead attempting to solve problems. The mediator has no power; rather, the mediator is a facilitator helping each party articulate his or her needs, clarify the issues and reach agreements. We encourage all parties to listen to each other and initially talk about issues and needs, not positions or solutions. We need to focus on those issues we can control or are empowered to handle.

Future versus past orientation: In this, the mediator explains we are not so interested in who has done what to whom, but in how we want things different in the future. At times, examples of past difficulties may be discussed, as a way to clear up misinterpretations or perceptions. Mediation recognizes that there have been unsuccessful attempts in the past to problem-solve, and the job at hand is to create new answers to old problems.

One at a time with no interrupting: This ground rule is very important for mediators to establish. While it may sound very elementary, it isn't. People have a natural tendency to explain or defend themselves if they perceive they are being attacked or misunderstood or if their emotions get the better of them. When someone interrupts, the mediator needs to stop him and remind him that all parties will get a chance to tell their stories. This may have to be said more than once. If you are a participant in the process and someone interrupts you, gently remind him that all agreed to let each party speak uninterrupted.

Time limits: Time limits for specific segments of discussion should be negotiated up front and adhered to. This shows respect for all parties involved and their time and helps to achieve buy-in. Be advised that someone undoubtedly will attempt to bring up an issue at the last minute. The last few minutes should be a recap of what was discussed and perhaps agreed upon, and can be used for planning the next session.

Consequences of reaching no agreement: The mediator or the parties themselves may want to discuss what the likely outcomes may be if no agreement is reached. In divorce mediation, the mediator may advise the couple that if they do not solve the problems in mediation, that the next step may be a judge deciding for them. At work, if two departments cannot work the problem out, it may be the supervisor deciding. Or in the family, Mom or Dad might advise the kids that if mediation fails, they, as parents, will decide who does what chores. This is not threatening, but merely discussing the natural consequences of the parties failing to reach agreement.

Only one party can be mad at a time: Sometimes humor can help break the initial tension that will naturally be present in these sessions. Tell the parties involved that only one can be mad at a time. It will help lighten things up and recognize that the tension exists. However, use good judgement in attempting to inject humor. It can backfire if the perception is given that you don't care or are not taking the issues seriously.

PHASE III:
IDENTIFYING ISSUES

After the stage is set, the next step is to *identify all the issues* important to the parties. If you are the mediator, simply call on one of the parties to begin. If you are a participant, let the other party go first. Parents may want to let the children speak first. This may be something new in your family, but it shows that you respect them. If you do this, they are more likely to listen to you after you have listened to them first. The following principles will help to facilitate mutual identification of and agreement on the issues.

Venting/story-telling: Each party needs to be able to vent uninterrupted, getting their thoughts and feelings off their chests in front of all the parties involved. In essence, they need to tell their stories. Telling their stories has a cathartic effect, in that people usually feel better after they have vented in a safe environment. All parties, having heard the honest thoughts and feelings of others, can begin to appreciate how others perceive the issues and how the issues impact them. The party telling her story also can hear and evaluate, maybe for the first time, her own thoughts and perceptions.

Reflective listening: Whether you are in the role of mediator or participant, reflective listening can help you encourage the story-telling and communicate your understanding of the issues. If the party telling their story is talkative, passive listening works well. As someone is talking, a few "Uh-huh's" or eye contact with a few head nods will accomplish the task. If the other party is not particularly talkative, eye contact and silence can be used to encourage them to communicate. As you listen for the issues, reflect back on what you hear with statements such as "Sounds like that's important to you," "Seems that how we communicate is a big issue for you" or "When I don't talk to you first, you feel I'm going behind your back?"

Issue identification: As each party tells their story, listen carefully for what seem to be major points or issues. Sometimes participants will bring concrete issues to the table. If this is the case, issue identification is a matter of understanding participants' issues, helping to ensure that their issues are reflective of the situation. Narrow the focus so that each issue is defined well enough to be workable. Sometimes parties will bring feelings to the table. Feelings may be generalized, with attitudes such as, "This family stinks" or "This department is a mess." Rather than attend to the feelings, attempt to remove them and help the party clarify the issues. Reflective listening and open-ended questions can be used to do this. Ask questions such as, "Sounds like you feel very strongly about the family's situation; what exactly do you feel stinks?" or "I can understand that you feel the department is in chaos, but what is it that you see?" For mediators and participants alike, the task at hand is to help all parties define their issues.

As you ask open-ended questions, reflect feelings and help narrow down the issues. Paraphrasing each party's issues will help to clarify the issues and create buy-in for all. Make comments such as, "Seems to me, based on what you're saying, that the chaos in the department is due, in part, to a lack of face-to-face communication" or "Your unhappiness with the family appears to be caused by us (parents) always telling you what to do." The party will either agree or disagree. If the party responds with "Yeah, that's right, bingo, exactly," then the issue has been correctly identified. If not, continue to paraphrase or ask questions that require the party to zero in on the issue.

Issue consensus: Whether you are participant or mediator, always listen for any areas of agreement as the issues are clarified. In the role of mediator, look for common issues and comment on them. For example, if you hear all parties identifying that how they talk to each other is a common issue, you can say, "Sounds like how you treat each other verbally is an issue for everybody in the department, including management." As a participant, listen to the other parties' issues, notice how close they might be to yours and comment on them. Chances are they are roughly the same. For example, in the family, if the kids' issue is that you yell too much and you think the kids are disrespectful at times, try a comment like, "Seems like one of the issues we share is how we all talk to each other."

Always listen for issues common to all and get consensus. Most parties involved in dispute resolution will try to sharpen their differences, initially. After all, it is the differences that have caused the difficulties. But this sets a negative tone to the mediation and can block the entire process of getting agreements. Momentum is important in dispute resolution, especially when issues are numerous. It doesn't make any sense to initially emphasize how far apart parties are. Instead, start with how close they are or what they seem to have in common. This, then, can set a positive tone and help participants see that their issues actually are solvable.

As you clarify and reach consensus on the major issues, you are creating an allegiance with the parties involved. This is another form of "transitioning," in which we begin to transition away from a position where we see each other as the problem to a position where we see the *issues* as the problem. Therefore, the parties are coming together to deal with a common enemy (issues). Ury (1992) in his book, *Getting Past No,* calls this the side-by-side strategy of negotiation. Rather than face-off against another party, you invite them to your side to help deal with the common problems. Work groups consisting of employees and management transition away from blaming each other to rallying together to tackle their problems. Family members transition away from perceiving each other as uncaring or hostile and focus their collective energies on how to deal differently with their common problems.

Every now and then a party will have an issue that others do not share, or more likely, do not see as important. These issues can't be ignored. Good mediators never argue over whether a concern is an issue or not, nor its relative importance. In an ongoing relationship, if one party has an issue, it is an issue to all and must be respected as such by all.

At a large Midwestern manufacturing company, we were asked to mediate a series of issues between employees and management. An attitude and opinion survey had indicated that wage rates were a major issue among employees. Management was upset and felt their wage concern was ridiculous. The employees were well paid and should be grateful. They didn't think that the wages should be an issue. When the two groups tried to talk about it on their own, they just became angry with one another.

Rather than mediate, it was suggested that if it was a fact that the employees were well-paid, management needed to demonstrate that fact to their employees and not discount their perceptions. A committee of management and employees conducted a salary survey of comparable positions. The result of the survey indicated that the wages ranked in the 89th percentile. After the committee discovered this key piece of information, wages were no longer an issue. In addition, management learned never to dismiss another party's issue. Rather, they learned what everyone should remember, include the other party's issues and help develop ways to deal with it. This also enhances relationships by demonstrating your concern and caring.

PHASE IV:
REFRAME ISSUES

Once issues have been identified and consensus established, the groundwork needs to be laid for getting agreements. To do so, the issues must be further defined or *reframed* into needs. This transforms the negotiations into a needs-based negotiation. In our experience, we've found that most issues can be reframed into the following needs:

Empowerment/respect: With this need, parties often feel that their thoughts or needs don't matter. Most people need some input or control regarding their lives or work. They need to feel valued and empowered to give input and make some decisions. When agreements pay attention to empowerment/respect needs, all parties become stakeholders; they have ownership, and the likelihood of compliance with the agreements improves.

Trust: Parties at times may feel they cannot believe one or all of the others involved. In an ongoing relationship all parties have trust needs, whether they are parent-child, peer-peer, management-employee or nation-nation. If trust is a need, a good agreement will reflect this need in detailing how this need will be met.

Communication: Parties often feel that how they communicate is not productive, that it is inflammatory, adversarial or nonexistent. In business or families, Codes of Conduct (Chapter 8) can be established. How parties communicate is just as important, if not more, than the agreements reached. If the parties can communicate effectively, almost any issue can be worked out.

Truth/Honesty: Parties sometimes feel they were lied to, or more commonly, have misperceived another party's statements or actions. Needs that focus on truth and honesty are sometimes cleared up in the mediation process as all parties tell their stories, identify their issues and look at their needs. Negative assumptions and misperceptions can be exposed and explained. Regardless, the need for truth and honesty should be addressed for any agreement to be long-lasting.

Turn negative statements into need based statements: Negotiations can break down or turn hostile when parties begin making negative statements to each other. Sometimes negative words, barbs, digs or attacking statements will elicit equally negative statements, or worse, from others. It is the skillful mediator, participant, parent or coach who can take that negative statement and turn it into a needs-based statement.

Just as we discussed in the chapter on communication and constructive confrontation, rather than attack in retaliation or refuse to participate, we need to throw out, or ju-jitsu, the emotion and identify the need embedded in the emotion. For example, if a mediation participant were to say, "Well you are such a back-stabber and gossip. At least I don't do that!" we shouldn't respond with a negative comment about her. Instead ask, "To work better together, you need for me to be honest and tell you what I think, not others?"

After that party agrees, you then can identify a need such as, "I can try coming to you first with a problem, but I need to feel you are willing to listen and not get angry." As the mediator, you might respond to the same statement with, "Seems that honesty (removing the words back stabber and gossip) is a big need for you. How do others feel about honesty in this department?"

Just about any negative statement can be turned into a needs-based statement:

Business	**Family**
• That department never helps us out during peak times (you need everyone to pitch in).	• I'm sick of Jennifer always getting her way (you need to be treated equally).
• We're sick of the gossip that's spread around here (you need people to refrain from spreading rumors.)	• I have to do all the work around here (you need a fair work schedule).
• I feel like I'm taking orders from peers, and I don't have a say (you need some control).	• No one listens to what I say (you need to be heard and acknowledged).

PHASE V:
GETTING AGREEMENTS

The final phase of the mediation process is *getting agreements*. At times, some parties will try to offer or impose solutions while in the issue or reframing phases. Resist this, as it is premature. All issues need to be identified and needs explored. All parties need a chance to tell their stories for the best agreements to be developed.

Solutions/agreements: Once issues and needs have been identified and consensus achieved, it is now time to funnel up; that is, to begin the process of generating multiple possible solutions from participants based on the issues and needs that were expressed. You can make statements such as, "Based on the issues you all have identified and the needs you have, what can you think of in terms of solutions that meet these needs?" or "What ideas can we come up with to deal with our issues that also pay attention to our needs?"

At times, even though the negotiations have been issue-based and needs based, some parties will offer a position that seemingly only meets their needs. Rather than argue over their positions, simply say, "What else can you think of?" or "Help me understand how this idea meets everyone's needs and addresses the issues on the table." By continuing to ask, "What else can you think of?" you put the responsibility back on the parties to generate multiple options to solve the problems and thus increase the likelihood of finding one or more that all parties can live with.

Offer suggestions: As the mediator you can offer suggestions or food for thought to entice the parties to examine other alternatives. If you are an experienced mediator, you may know how similar problems have been solved elsewhere, and it is fine to offer suggestions. Keep in mind that a mediator cannot impose a solution, nor should he lead parties to a solution. To do so without imposing, you can make statements such as "I'm wondering if you have ever considered ..." or "Other groups in your same situation have tried ...." Offering suggestions is merely intended to stimulate discussion, not make decisions for parties.

At one Mental Health Center, we were asked to help key staff and management identify issues and needs. We offered the idea of establishing a joint task force, which had worked well with a previous client. They took the suggestion and decided during the task force meeting to train all staff in confrontation and mediation techniques. They developed codes of conduct and even instituted peer mediation so they could deal with their own problems without necessarily having to involve management or the grievance procedure. And their solutions met their needs for empowerment and communication ... all because of a simple suggestion.

Objective criteria: Another strategy that helps in needs-based negotiation is to collect and consider objective criteria. At times, if parties in mediation are having a hard time generating solutions or agreements, can they at least agree to some measurement or benchmark that could help come to an agreement? Could the work group benchmark with similar and dissimilar groups to see how they handle the same problems? Could the family agree to ask a counselor what might be appropriate privileges for a 14-year-old? Could a couple agree to consult a financial adviser to determine how much money needs to be saved each month for college educations? If the parties can't come to an agreement, would they agree to a process that could render a solution? Keep in mind that this process is not binding arbitration, in which one side wins and the other loses. It is agreeing to some form of outside measurement to aid in decision-making.

Grab agreements: As agreements are reached, grab them. As soon as the parties say, "I could live with that," "That idea would meet my needs and deal with the issues" or "We could try that," grab that agreement and move on to the next issue or end the mediation. To do so, either as a participant or mediator, you simply restate the agreement and ask if your interpretation is correct. If so, then it needs to be documented, in writing, on the spot, to be included in a memorandum of agreement or written action plan. Don't belabor the agreement or play devil's advocate by asking "What if ..." questions. Just get the agreement down and move on.

Memorandum of agreement or action plan: All successful mediations need to be summarized in writing. In divorce or family mediation, agreements need to be recorded in what's called a memorandum of agreement. A good memorandum of agreement usually is prefaced by a paragraph or so stating that the following agreements were based on our mutual respect for each other and need for ongoing open communication, even though at times we may disagree. This helps bond the agreements to the ongoing relationship with each other and codifies efforts to reach agreements that meet everyone's needs.

In business, an action plan needs to be drawn up that details the agreements reached. Usually this is done along with a code of conduct. The action plan needs to spell out the agreements reached, as well as who is going to do what and by when. For example, if one of the agreements reached was to form a joint task force of employees and management to institute a peer mediation program, questions such as who is responsible and when will it be accomplished must be answered in the action plan. If agreed to by all parties, union contracts can be rewritten to include agreements reached in mediation or even to include the mediation process in contract negotiations.

If no agreements are reached: Even the most skillful mediator or participant at times will be unable to get agreements. At least you tried. And at least you demonstrated your willingness to participate. This may leave the door open for some future opportunity to try again. Some parties will just refuse to let go of the past or are so convinced that they are right that they are willing to sacrifice the relationship to prove it. Driving through an intersection, you may have the right-of-way. But if the other person isn't going to stop, you may need to to avoid a collision.

If no agreements are reached, more traditional processes can be initiated, such as the grievance procedure, a strike, lock-out, litigation, asking someone to make the decision for you or waging war. Sometimes you may get a partial agreement. Or if no concrete agreements were reached, you can agree to try again. If so, consider this a success. No system, process or technique works every time. At the very least, if you follow these steps and make a genuine effort, you can tell yourself when you go to sleep at night that you've done everything possible to enhance your relationships.

INTERNATIONAL AND UNION MEDIATION – CAN IT BE DONE?

Is it possible to have countries mediate rather than negotiate? It would seem that the process could easily be applied. Ground rules would still need to be established. A facilitator would need to make sure that the past is past and that the emphasis is on the future. There would have to be a perception of a level playing field–that both countries, or all countries, would be "persuade-able" and willing to give up positions.

Issues would still be identified and expressed as needs. Each country would tell its story. Techniques and processes, such as leveling, still would need to be used. The mediator would look for areas of agreement. Hopefully there would be a transition from "us versus them" to "us against the issues."

Countries, like people, want respect, honesty, communication and trust. Eventually, agreements can be reached; and hopefully they are agreements that countries are more committed to because they had basic needs met in developing them.

Unions, too, could mediate issues. It is a different way to look at what traditionally has been a win/lose strategy or a compromise style. Normally both parties decide what their positions are, what is the least they will give in to and the least they will accept, and then go back and give something up to settle for some things at a lesser degree than they wanted. Why couldn't both parties meet, hold off on the positions, talk about needs and look for shared interests? Maybe it is because that often times the issues are only part of the dynamic that takes place at those tables. Many times there is wounding from things that have gone on in previous years at the bargaining table or in the workplace and the negotiation session becomes a time to "get those guys for what we've had to put up with."

Now you see how important it is to preserve the quality of an ongoing relationship with people and with the union in your company. When the relationship is there, there is no problem in meeting everyone's needs, because we realize that in meeting the company's needs, the union benefits; and the company realizes that if the union is happy, we have better products or services.

When we disagree, we can agree to look at objective criteria and compromise. At the least, the negotiations are easier when trust, honesty, communication and respect have taken place on a daily basis. Then and only then will all parties feel that it is in everyone's best interest to reach honorable and equitable agreements that meet everyone's needs. When there is a relationship of trust, good things happen for both parties.

We had the pleasure of working with two groups in particular that asked us to help both the union and the management in making negotiations run better. In one group, we introduced the concept of needs-based negotiation to representatives of both the union and management. The result was that the following year's negotiation went better.

In another case, we helped the union with a retraining issue. The tolerances of parts manufactured were inconsistent shift to shift. That frustrated even the members of the union. After getting together, they decided to cross-train the machinists, something that was a hot topic at their last negotiation. Management was very pleased, and the union only decided to do this because THEY made the decision. They weren't told to do it by the management. As we have maintained throughout this book, relationships are foundational to all aspects of the organization, family or country. Anything that can be done to improve relationships improves everything.

MEDIATION AND COACHING

The same components of mediation are used in the coaching process. Issues are identified after ground rules are established. Assessments are performed to help with the issues. The needs of both the company and the person being coached are expressed. Leveling is used, if needed. In areas of shared interest, solutions are identified, and a code of conduct and action plan are established. Instruction is given on how to achieve the items in the action plan and code. In some cases, role playing and modeling take place to help with practice of the processes. Follow-up takes place to reinforce changed behavior and make sure there is accountability.

In all the cases mentioned, alternative dispute resolution is an excellent process for enhancing relationships while solving problems, a process that pays high dividends after it occurs for all the parties involved and the company or country that was enlightened enough to use it.

CHAPTER SEVEN

Key Points to Consider:

- Look for needs rather than positions.

- Funnel *up*, not *down*, to be creative and generate multiple solutions.

- Determine first if mediation is appropriate.

- If appropriate, remember to:
  1. Make the considerations.
  2. Set the stage.
  3. Identify the issues.
  4. Reframe the issues.
  5. Grab agreements.

- Mediate rather than negotiate.

Harnessing The Power of Conflict

CHAPTER EIGHT

CODE OF CONDUCT

Most companies have written job descriptions for all employees. Business puts a lot of effort into mission and vision statements. Progressive industries hire outside consultants to help develop strategic plans. Human resource departments spend countless hours developing policy and procedure manuals. Almost all companies have elaborate grievance procedures, detailing the levels to go to and the time lines for responses. One organization we know of has a policy on how to wash your hands (and to think, all these years we may have been doing this incorrectly!). But rarely do companies have a policy on how to communicate. Enter any break area, and you'll see:

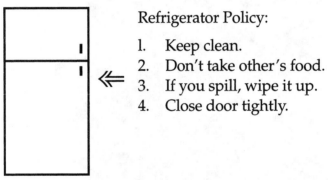

Refrigerator Policy:

1.   Keep clean.
2.   Don't take other's food.
3.   If you spill, wipe it up.
4.   Close door tightly.

Considering that everyone owns one, if they don't know these things by now, we have problems!

What we need is a procedure on communication that is at least as detailed and hopefully less insulting than the refrigerator policy. It would be a policy developed by the employees or families so they can buy into it. It would be a policy that encourages people to solve problems at the lowest levels possible. It would reduce gossip and back-stabbing and increase communication. It would be a policy or contract written by a group for the group called a CODE OF CONDUCT.

Companies and families often have unwritten codes of conduct. In a company, these are often defined by the corporate culture. The more authoritarian the culture, the more the unwritten code of conduct encourages people to keep their mouths shut, not to rock the boat and not to lose their jobs. Here is an unwritten code of conduct:

UNWRITTEN
CODE OF CONDUCT

1. Don't confront anyone.

2. If you do confront, rip the other person to shreds.

3. Don't discuss single issues: wait and collect them like green stamps, and cash them in when you have a full book.

4. Make sure you tell others rather than the person involved.

5. Break times, lunch or after work are good times to talk about others behind their backs.

6. Anger and rage are fine ways of expressing yourself.

7. Keep quiet and internalize your frustrations.

8. Be competitive with others and win...let them lose.

9. Be suspicious and mistrusting. Just because you're paranoid doesn't mean everyone isn't out to get you.

10. Don't share ideas. Nothing ever changes anyway, and you might lose your job.

For some, this code of conduct looks familiar. If you polled parents or managers, many would say that dealing with conflict takes up a lot of time and that it's a task they really don't enjoy. The problem is that they don't have a proactive, mutually agreed upon method to handle conflict. If there isn't a method in writing, then the unwritten code of conduct takes over.

A code of conduct is not a grievance procedure. Grievance procedures are last-resort efforts that encourage employees to continue to argue or to have someone else make a decision for them. When someone makes a decision for us and acts as a judge, we are frequently not happy with the decision, because it isn't our decision.

When people are asked to work things out on their own, the question is HOW? If they had the skills or methodology to do so, they would have worked it out already. Simply asking people to solve problems on their own tends to encourage them to fail. When management and parents make decisions in this manner–the manner used by our legal system–they create winners and losers. Instead, a written code of conduct creates winners and winners.

Codes of conduct are developed before action planning. Writing your code of conduct before you begin action planning fosters better buy-in for the entire process. Not only does this sequence help people to be understood, but it provides them with necessary skills before they are asked to commit to the code of conduct.

To write a code of conduct, it is often helpful to have the group list perceptions they see operating currently. The opposites of those behaviors, if negative, are then listed. Subsequently the group is asked how they can move from point A to point B. The resulting discussion leads to the development of the code of conduct.

One company did that in this way:

A		**B**
Current Perceptions		**Desired Reality**
Mistrust	⇛	Trust
Competition	⇛	Teamwork
Paranoia	⇛	Confidence
Anger	⇛	Peace
Deceit	⇛	Honesty
Win/Lose	⇛	Win/Win
Gossiping	⇛	One-to-One Personal Communication

All codes of conduct are individualized for the organization or family writing them, but many of them have the same elements as this company had.

Similar to the workplace, an unwritten code of conduct exists in our homes. In a family, it may look something like this:

UNWRITTEN CODE OF CONDUCT

1. When someone is bothering us, make sure we tattle to Mom or Dad.

2. If Dad comes home angry, leave him alone until he is happy again.

3. When angry with each other, we will give each other the silent treatment.

4. The children are great verbal punching bags in case we are having a bad day and need to take our frustrations out on people who won't fight back or threaten us.

5. Choose sides with the children and punish one when they are fighting.

Perhaps a *written* family code of conduct might look differently. It may have some rules that Dad and/or Mom put in and some rules the children put in. Some might be made together. (This is not meant to sound old-fashioned. No one is suggesting that the family will become the Cleaver household of the 1950s.) But talking to one another and building a family communication contract, or a code of conduct, helps everyone to understand what the rules are so that they can live with respect for one another. It is particularly useful in blended family households.

A written code of conduct for families might look like this:

CODE OF CONDUCT
FOR THE JOHNSON FAMILY

1. Kids can try to confront each other before bringing problems to Mom and Dad.

2. Parents will not take out frustration on the children.

3. If Dad is angry, he will tell us why and then make efforts to calm down.

4. We will speak up and say what is on our mind to each other.

5. We will encourage the children to work things out on their own and if they can't, then we will intervene.

6. We will listen to the children without interrupting.

7. We will discuss decisions before rendering a vedict.

Whether in a business or in a family, a code of conduct helps set the rules straight before people violate them, which enhances communication and strengthens relationships. Most people don't mind following rules if they are known in advance, if they are applied consistently and if they are fair.

An example of a written code of conduct for a company looks like this:

CODE OF CONDUCT

1. Use leveling and positive confrontation.

2. Agree to communicate directly, one to one.

3. Be receptive to positive confrontation.

4. Be aware of differing perspectives.

5. Check out perceptions for accuracy.

6. Direct others back to the source; don't participate in or listen to gossip.

A code of conduct also is used in the coaching process. As you see in the coaching chapter, there are assessments used and a type of issue identification to diagnose the areas where work is needed. After the goals are established and coaching is nearing completion, a method to continue the desired behaviors is needed to ensure that the corrected behaviors do not become extinguished. The code of conduct is one of two methods used. Codes of conduct outline HOW the person will interact with others. Action plans, discussed in Chapter 9, outline WHAT the person will do to achieve success in the future. An example of a Code of Conduct in Coaching might look like this (notice that the 3-4 points deal with HOW the person will interact with others–less is more):

Use leveling to deal with conflicts as they arise when interacting with others.

Listen to people before giving my opinion.

Involve people in decision making before giving my final answer.

Communicate personal information so that people do not view me as cold or aloof.

CHAPTER EIGHT

Key Points to Consider:

- A code of conduct is a policy designed by staff for staff that outlines an agreement how people will interact with each other.

- Families can also establish codes of conduct.

- Unwritten codes of conduct operate unless written ones replace them.

- Codes of conduct outline how we will agree to interact before issues arise.

Harnessing The Power of Conflict

CHAPTER NINE

ACTION PLANNING, FIRST STEPS AND FOLLOW-UP MEETINGS

All too often, work groups or families will identify issues either among themselves, with supervisors or with outside consultants or counselors and never follow up with action steps. We ask, "What good does it do to go to a doctor, find out you have an infection, get a prescription, and then never take it?" If you don't take the medication, you won't get better. Groups work the same way. There must be commitment from the members to take action steps toward carrying out the code of conduct. And there must be support from those in authority. Then these techniques will not be just another false start, another program that makes employees feel good for only a few days before behaviors degenerate back into business as usual.

At the beginning of action planning, employees or families must recognize the importance of separating issues into two groups: those over which they have control and those over which they don't.

Why worry about things you can't impact? If we've learned to recognize and influence our perceptions (how we view things); we understand there is no need to waste time waiting for others to change.

In our sessions, we encourage people to select the top five issues over which they have control. These become the issues for which they will plan a strategy. Group members must realize they have the most control over themselves and each other and begin to take ownership rather than looking upward to make things better. When this occurs, they are ready to make the changes necessary to improve. Some people may not be committed totally to the process. Even so, behavior will improve, as long as the group adheres to its code of conduct and refuses to let a few people negatively influence the whole group. If there is no one in management, on the board or among the staff who will listen, trouble-makers will stop distracting. A wise woman once said, "If someone is griping too much, someone else is listening too much."

The best way to make progress at this critical juncture is just to let the group move forward. If the majority of a group is committed to making things work, the few who are not will not spoil the progress.

In selecting only the top five issues, we're recognizing that not all the issues identified need to be addressed. The famous Pareto Principle holds true here, as well. If 20 percent of our key issues are addressed, 80 percent of our problems will be resolved. The group needs to let go of the issues over which they have no control (i.e., hours, pay, food, staffing, equipment purchases, floor space and the personal qualities of management, administration, parents or siblings). Instead, they need to focus on things they can impact. And they usually need only to focus on the major ones.

In a company, it may be beneficial to break a larger group down into subgroups and have them rank order the issues, arriving at the top five issues over which they have control. The lists of all the groups can then be brought together and ranked. A consensus list of the top five issues is now available. If there are more than five issues that the group agrees need to be addressed, they may choose to do so.

Concurrently, as the group is discussing the top issues, they need to be encouraged to develop action steps for addressing those issues. They only need to write down one or two steps necessary to begin to deal with the issues. Writing down a 25-page action plan for each step usually becomes a useless writing activity. All the effort is placed in development of the plan, with no energy reserved to carry it out. Most people have enough work to do without coming up with an elaborate action plan that does nothing but set them up for failure when they find they cannot accomplish it all. By developing these first few steps, they become empowered to decide what they want to do.

In business, action planning often is conducted in a follow-up meeting. Management frequently is invited to attend. The employees can be working on identifying their top five issues and action steps for their issues, while the management works on doing the same thing for issues that employees identified for management to work on. When this occurs, it really empowers employees and helps make the management team an integral part of the solution. It shows employees that all members of the team are committed to making the process work. And it breaks down we-they barriers and gets everyone functioning together for the betterment of the department or company.

Follow-up meetings become a check on the progress of the code of conduct and Action Plan. Employees and managers can discuss what is working and what isn't. Fine-tuning can take place. Retraining can occur as necessary. New people can be oriented to the process, the code of conduct and the action plan. The next steps of the action plan can be identified and carried out.

Our process is ongoing. Groups must continually rework the action plan so that it does not become outdated. If it isn't the type of document that is used, redone and used again, it will become extinct; and like other things that have become extinct, it will disappear and be forgotten. Forgotten things are of no use to a work team.

An example of a corporation's action plan and first steps for staff and managers might look like this:

STAFF ACTION PLAN/FIRST STEPS

Issue	Action Plan
1. Gossip/back-stabbing	a. Direct people back to the person concerned.
	b. Refer to code of conduct.
	c. Don't talk about people except to them.
	d. Use leveling, not gossip.
2. No time to problem-solve	a. Use 15 minutes of staff meeting for brainstorming problems/solutions.
	b. Hold potluck lunch once a month to speak with management about problems.
	c. Make each employee responsible forone action item and report each month on progress.

SUPERVISORS ACTION PLAN/FIRST STEPS

Issue	Action Plan
1. Unapproachable	a. Maintain regular office hours 1x/week.
	b. Use confrontation, not yelling.
	c. Invite each employee in for meeting in addition to performance review.
	d. Attend staff functions when invited, on all shifts.

When groups develop their own action plans, they are committed to carrying them out. At work, employees become stakeholders. They are much more likely to carry out the plans and adhere to the Code of Conduct because they developed it, rather than someone from above developing it for them.

In business, it is recommended that follow-up meetings are held for the first year after going through intervention. This helps to fine-tune and update the process, to teach new people and to regenerate interest in the process.

Meetings for staff and management usually are held one month after the initial mediation to review mediation techniques that build on the communication process.

More role playing can be done at this time (and the importance of role plays cannot be stressed enough). Role plays lay new tracks for people who have developed habits they need to change. If there are parts of the process that don't seem to be working, they can be fine-tuned in role playing.

What is the prognosis for long-term success? The prognosis is good if people stay committed and focused. It is important that ample reinforcement is given to work groups that undergo such tremendous retooling. These groups have taken monumental risk, have exhibited courage, and have spent volumes of energy in turning themselves around. If they are not encouraged and supported by a company, then the company deserves what it gets.

If a company is mired in dysfunction, people at higher levels may not want to have a group out there that is different from the rest. But when a company is healthy, those at the top support and encourage work groups and teams who are self-sufficient, self-correcting and self-actualized. They also support groups that use the methods so that they can deal with staff members not as controlling parents, but as team members whose mutual support and cooperation is necessary for everyone to succeed. Groups must have these qualities at their foundation before such programs as continuous quality improvement teams or high performance

SELF MEDIATING WORK TEAMS   self-actualized

self-sufficient

self-correcting

teams stand a chance of succeeding. When groups are self-sufficient, self-correcting and self actualized, they can do anything.

FAMILY CONTRACTS

At home, a family contract incorporates the same principles. It's important for the family to get together and mutually identify the top issues they think stand in the way of their being able to communicate and interact effectively with one another. They can then brainstorm some methods to deal with those ineffective behaviors. And they should break those methods into steps. Once they have successfully incorporated those new behaviors into daily life, they can go on to identify more issues and action steps to eliminate those problems.

A family action plan contract may look like this:

Issue		Action Step
1. **Tattling** (child to child)	a.	We tell Mom and Dad only things that people are doing that might harm them or others.
	b.	We try to work it out first and then go to Mom or Dad if we can't.
	c.	Mom and Dad will try to help us decide and not make all of our decisions for us.
2. **Short with Kids** (child to parent)	a.	We will listen until the kids are finished talking.
	b.	We count to five before giving a response.
	c.	Responses are not sarcastic, even if we think the question is silly.
	d.	If we can't be interrupted or if we're angry, we take a "time out" and discuss things later.
3. **Lack of Support** (parent to parent)	a.	We can disagree, but in private.
	b.	We support each other's decisions.
	c.	We ask the child if the other parent has been asked and a decision made before we tell the child yes or no.

Remember, if only 20 percent of the issues are resolved, the family unit functions much better. In a single-parent household, the parent can have the same contract with the children. Special circumstances (i.e., the child begins dating, the child begins to drive, the child coming back from college with younger children in the house is still expected to do chores) may warrant a contract. It's a great way to enhance communication and get agreement on what to do. This empowers all family members and thus, helps all become more willing to adhere to the rules.

Action plans for coached employees again, should deal with WHAT needs to be accomplished. The code of conduct addresses HOW things should be accomplished, or the interpersonal side of the equation. Both the code of conduct and action plan can be combined into one document, with no more than five to eight items initially listed as to-do steps. Others can be added after the employee experiences success with those first steps. If an employee refuses to do the code and action plan, or does one and fails to attempt to adhere to it, then these items can be used as documentation of the organization's attempt at intervention before further disciplinary action is taken. But if someone tries and fails, support should still be given. Growth occurs from making mistakes. It's lack of effort or sabotage of the plan that would warrant discipline. Remember, we don't make changes unless the heat is turned up, so to speak. So struggle can be a good thing, helping people become motivated to overcome the struggle, either on their own or with and through others, if they need to.

The action plan would look something like this in the coaching area:

ACTION PLAN FOR BOB SMITH

1. Change the format of meetings to include time for information sharing and time for discussion that leads to decisions.
2. Rotate tasks so that all employeoes feel they have a chance to work on exciting an dless exciting jobs equally.
3. Begin attending the staff meetings of those who report to me, to increase visibility.
4. Give regular feedback to Sherie, my supervisor.

CHAPTER NINE

Key Points to Consider:

- Action planning is used by people to outline what steps they should take to correct their own issues.

- Write only a few action steps for each of your top five issues.

- Follow-up meetings maintain commitment.

Harnessing The Power of Conflict

CHAPTER TEN

COACHING

We have all seen coaches at a football or basketball game. They pace back and forth with a clipboard, looking at the whole picture and making notes. During a time-out, they attempt to correct problems that those playing the game cannot see. Before the game, they plan, go over strategies with the players and run drills to give the players practice. During the game, they watch, they correct, they support. After the game, they review and correct for next time. Coaches help bring out the best in the athlete for the good of the team, with both benefiting from the experience.

Coaches in business do the same sort of things. They help individuals and the company at the same time. For the individual, they offer assessment, guidance, feedback and planning to help the client to be more successful. Moreover, coaches help clients identify and change self-defeating thoughts and behaviors that inhibit their performance or the performance of the company.

For the company, the coach helps people who the company feels it needs to retain. These might be highly compensated executives or key professionals in whom the company has invested time and training and does not want to let go without making an attempt at correcting behaviors it wants changed. The behaviors are usually interpersonal in nature, and hamper the individual's ability to manage, succeed or lead **highly effective** teams. They may have the technical skills, but lack the interpersonal skills or team skills to work well with peers, superiors or subordinates.

We coach employees because it makes sense to develop talent we already have, to correct some of the problems with people who already know the culture and policies and mission of the organization. We coach to give people another chance at changing unwanted behaviors. We coach because it is less expensive than recruiting and hiring and orienting and developing outside talent. We don't always know what we are getting from the outside. The talent pool of outside candidates is a lot like the people who are already working for the organization. In other words, they ARE who you HAVE. The new person from the outside, though maybe more talented in certain ways, brings with her or him some flaws, as well. Everyone has issues to deal with. The question is, are they a fit in your culture? Can their weaknesses be controlled, or are they even a weakness in our culture? Can they develop, learn and grow? Are they a match? Do they have the interpersonal skills needed to work with your people, with your teams? These are key questions we must ask before hiring someone.

We often think there is a pool of excellent people "out there," if only we could find one or two of them. It's like a football or baseball team that picks up some expensive free agents only to find they were not the answer for their team. Yes, on their previous team, they were stars; but here, they are not a match.

It makes good business sense to keep and develop employees that are already on board. Business recognized this concept in the 1940s, when employee assistance programs began to emerge as a benefit in corporations. Business saved money helping employees help themselves with alcoholism, mental illness and family problems. Not only did it make financial sense, but also ethically it became the right thing to do. Coaching is another avenue that can make good employees better.

We define coaching as: "A planned intervention with an individual to enhance or remediate skill sets necessary to optimally function or succeed in his leadership position." Enhancement would be coaching those individuals where the individual or company desires to:

• Hone the leadership skills of high-potential individuals within the company.

• Provide management and interpersonal skills for highly technical-oriented employees.

• To support the growth and success of newly promoted key personnel.

More often than not, this entails coaching those in leadership positions who:

- Have difficulty managing change.

- Have difficulty working in a team environment.

- Have poor interpersonal relations skills.

- Have under-performed and are headed for or involved in a disciplinary process in which coaching has been offered as an alternative to termination.

Who Are Coaches?

Who coaches? There is no universal or agreed upon formal training or licensure. Coaches should have psychological and interpersonal expertise, as well as proven business experience, to be able to help individuals become more successful. They are more than trainers, who can teach skills. They are more than consultants, who can offer different suggestions. They are more than mental health specialists who can diagnosis problems. They are more than ex-managers or executives who have decided to go into business for themselves. Effective coaches are all of the above with a vitae that includes proven business performance helping others realize their maximum potential.

Coaches may have different specialties. Like physicians or attorneys who specialize in one branch of medicine or the law, some coaches can help with financials, some with technical skills, some with planning and forecasting and some with interpersonal skills. As has been repeated in this book, the quality of the product or service you provide is dependent on the quality of working relationships. And the quality of the working relationships is dependent on the quality of interpersonal and communicative skills. We feel the interpersonal and communicative skills function is the most important. Without this component, a person who has high technical competence can still fail at his or her job.

Coaches can be from within the organization, and certainly a supervisor can act as a coach, but it is difficult for a supervisor to change roles from coach to authority figure. And the employee being coached might have a difficult time disclosing information of the sensitive nature to someone she or he reports to. So it is best left to people from the outside to coach. An external coach who is willing to spend the time to grasp the company's dynamics, mission, vision and culture is the best kind to secure.

The best way to approach coaching is to make it a requirement after all people at a certain level are hired, for the management team in total or for certain job classifications. Sometimes some level of coaching can be provided before it is needed. Part of the manager's or key person's orientation would include coaching with an outsider (with assessments) one to-ones, skill building, dialoging, networking and training to help that person succeed. Companies spend more money on balloons for the picnic than this would cost, and the yields would be phenomenal. But if this can't be done, at least coaching those who are having some difficulty makes sense.

It is important for the coach to spend time with managers, peers and sometimes subordinates and other key employees who interact with the employee being coached, as well as conducting individual coaching and assessment sessions. Usually follow-up sessions are held over time to strengthen and reinforce appropriate and desired behaviors, but that doesn't mean that a company should become dependent on consulting. We have all seen CEOs who have the "flavor-of-the-month" consultant in, not trusting her or his own decisions and direction, at great expense to the organization and much to the confusion of the managers and staff. Whose approach is the correct one, when 15 people are used in a year? Again, it makes sense to have different people for different needs and people who can deal with deficiencies in skill levels of upper management; but at some time, we have to trust our inner voice and make a decision, right or wrong, moving ahead with a course of action. We correct it if it is wrong and work with others, enlisting the talents and ideas of the good people we had the sense to hire. Yes, we go to the doctor when we are sick, and we even see specialists; but we don't need to go every month!

Every coach has her own approach, and every individual who wants or needs coaching is different. But we have found that successful coaching usually consists of some or all of the following components:

I. Information Gathering and Assessment

    a. The work environment and culture

    b. The client's self report

    c. Client assessment and testing, if necessary

II. Intervention

    a. Feedback from information gathering

    b. Goal-setting and building rapport

    c. Identification of self-defeating perceptions and behavior

    d. Discussion of strategies for goal attainment

I. Action Planning

    a. Code of conduct

    b. Action plan

    c. Follow-up

In the information gathering and assessment stage of coaching, a comprehensive picture of the client and his work environment is drawn. If the client is referred for coaching by upper management, a meeting is held with those managers. At that meeting, strengths and weaknesses as seen by the managers are discussed, as well as target behaviors for the client. As much information is gleaned regarding the corporate culture, mission and vision. It is usually helpful to meet with directors of human resources separately, as these professionals have invaluable information on how thing are really done in the company- and they have their fingers on the pulse of the organization.

Next comes a meeting with the client to determine how he sees himself in relationship to the work environment and his perceptions of his own strengths and weaknesses. Motivation to change and ownership of issues is assessed, and definition of the coaching relationship is discussed. We advise our clients that we are hired to help them be successful and that the company wants them to succeed. Otherwise we wouldn't be involved. Initially, most referred clients see coaching as punitive rather than helpful, so it is important to belay those fears. Depending on the information gathered and with the client's consent, meeting with staff who report to the client may be helpful in informing the client how he is perceived by their direct reports.

A physician we coached on his interpersonal skills spoke about how he resented being "taken to the woodshed" and having to be punished by seeing us. We explained that there was **basically** nothing wrong with him, and he didn't have to change his personality, as he had suggested the management wanted him to. We said, "Think of yourself like a person who has chosen to live overseas; we are here not to change you, but to show you the language and culture–to help you be happier and more successful." He had come from a very different corporate culture; and soon, the coaching helped him assimilate into his new culture, much to his surprise and the surprise of the staff that saw tremendous growth and change in him.

The coaching experience with this physician consisted of an initial meeting with the hospital administration and the nursing care managers who described their concerns regarding negative interactions with the doctor. Some particulars of this hospital's culture:

- Quality of the working relationships were stressed and cultivated.

- Consensus decisions were made when possible

- All team members were important.

- Socialization among different levels was promoted.

His previous hospital's culture said:

- We will be autocratic and silo functioning.

- Feelings are not important.

- Do your work and go home.

- Boundaries are very important.

As you can see, the conflict was apparent. After two coaching sessions that focused on leadership styles, interpersonal skills and dealing with perceptions (Chapters 5 & 6), he was able to get past "being taken to the woodshed," and set goals of a more collegial and democratic approach.

If the client is a self-referral (not referred by management for some problem), we see the client first to evaluate her needs and goals. Depending on the needs and goals, meetings with the client's employer may be appropriate.

Assessments or more formalized testing maybe appropriate. We have found the DISC to helpful in validating our observations, plus it provides a wealth of information on supervision and management styles of the client. The Meyers-Briggs also has proven helpful. We try to stay away from personality and projective testing.

In the intervention stage, a session is conducted with the client where he or she is gently confronted with all the information gathered. Negative and self-defeating perceptions are identified

(Chapter 5), challenged, and recommendations are given for skill acquisition or enhancement. Assessment data is interpreted. At this time, a <u>transition</u> usually occurs, in which the client accepts responsibility and eagerly moves to goal setting. Also, simultaneously, rapport is being established between the coach and client that further enhances and hastens the coaching experience.

Like the mediation of groups, coaching can utilize the components mentioned in this book. There is still issue identification, albeit by the individual, and a fact-finding caucus. There is still the use of brainstorming, leveling and reflective listening. However, a transition must still occur. In mediation, it occurs when a group sees that many of its issues to work on are the same as what it wants management to do. Here, it occurs when the client accepts that she must own some of the problem and resolve problems in interpersonal skills if she is going to be successful where she is or at any other organization. Needs are still identified by both the company and the individual. Shared needs are addressed by an action plan and code of conduct.

We worked with one manager who had problems relating to her staff. She had been hired from outside the organization. The organization was a tight group of people who had been there for a number of years. It was a small division of a larger company and had more small company values (we all go on break together, we are friends, we help each other, we meet socially after work, etc). Coming from one of the larger divisions, the manager was having great difficulty assimilating into a culture that was markedly different from her own experience (emotional detachment, rigid personal and professional boundaries). After about a month on the job, she fired a well-liked employee. After that, she was isolated, and soon, she made fewer and fewer attempts at getting along with the staff working for her. Pictures and nasty slogans were found attached to her computer screen. One day, she got into a verbal confrontation with one of her people, which resulted in her walking out on the employee. Her manager and VP of human resources then sent her to us.

We talked to her for a long time. But we sensed a lack of transition. She displaced blame on the employees and took on minimal responsibility for her own actions, even when confronted with her behavior directly. We then discussed the results of her DISC profile and showed her the results. She agreed with the profile, which said she was very dominant and aggressive, had little concern for people, did not like people to know anything about her personally, and could be perceived as aloof and impersonal. This helped us move forward. Finally, she could see how she was being perceived. As we have mentioned before, real or not, perceptions control the company. *A corporate culture is really shared perceptions.* If we want to change the culture, we have to change the way people think. We helped her develop an action plan to change the way people perceived her, without compromising who she was.

Some assessments can be very helpful in breaking the ice with the person being coached.

As in the above example, assessments can help a person transition. Just like groups transition when mediation is used, transition must happen on the interpersonal level if coaching is to be successful.

In action planning, a document is produced detailing what the client agrees to do in order to reach their goals. This may contain a code of conduct (Chapter 8), which would speak to <u>what</u> he is going to do, and/or an action plan (Chapter 9) that would detail <u>how</u> he is to interact more effectively with others to achieve optimum group performance. We have the client write his own action plan and will review it with him, making any recommendations deemed necessary. Follow up sessions to reinforce the changes, we believe, need to be on an as-needed basis. Certain coaching models suggest follow-up sessions need to occur on a regular basis. But as we stated previously, you don't want to become dependent on them.

The following action plan was developed by the client in our last example:

ACTION PLAN

1. Read the book, <u>Harnessing the Power of Conflict; Business and Family</u>. Incorporate applicable strategies and communication styles in an effort to promote change and motivation within my department.
(To be finished by 12/13/02)

2. Make it part of my daily routine to take about 15-20 minutes to wander and socialize a bit with fellow employees. It is important to notice personal things about them and make an effort to comment positively on things such as new hairdos, clothes, family pictures displayed. Be willing to reveal personal things about myself in an effort to form two-way conversations.
(Have initiated immediately)

3. Hold an initial "clear the air" meeting. Use diplomatic tools to convey to the department that it is recognized there are communication problems and take ownership of any of the issues specific to me. Have an open forum so anyone else can vent or offer suggestions for improvement.
(Meeting will be scheduled Week of 12/16)

4. Have regularly scheduled staff meetings and make them more "participative" in nature. Spend only 15 minutes on the information-sharing portion of the meeting and then leave the room, allowing the rest of the department about 30 to 45 minutes to review issues and basically take over the meeting among themselves to work on issues or resolutions to current problems. Have one team member keep notes of the meeting so that I can review and offer input, if needed. If they struggle to come up with any issues, approach an ally and ask him to come up with a topic for the next meeting and develop an agenda. Continue to leave the meeting so that they can handle the agenda.
(First meeting will be held week of January 6. Meetings will be weekly.)

5.   Make it a point to recognize positive accomplishments, no matter how small, and give positive feedback to the employees. Accentuate the positive more then the negative.
(On going)

6. Develop a thicker skin during the next two months or so understanding that there will be repercussion at first. It is likely to get worse before it gets better.
(On going)

As you can readily see this action plan is not a cradle-to-grave revamping of herself. We believe that most people just need help getting unstuck. Most people just lack certain skills and some self-insight needed to move to the next level. They don't need a 25-point strategic plan to change. Just like a company's mission and vision statement, the simpler the better. That's not to downplay results. We tell clients and client companies that with or without successful coaching, the employee is expected to perform.

The results must be beneficial for both the company and the individual. The code of conduct and action plan that the client develops can either be a tool to improve or documentation for the company that everything was attempted in order to intervene and change problem behaviors. If the client refuses to change–or, if after coaching, the behavior is still unacceptable–the company might have to proceed with further disciplinary action, but can do so with a clear conscience.

When you develop a talented person from within, it creates loyalty in that person. It shows the other employees that you are committed to their development, that you will go the extra mile to retain people who care and try, and that you invest in your people. Actions speak louder than words, and what a great way to build morale. Too often, the mission statement touts the importance of people as we brush them aside, hoping the new ones we hire are better than the old ones. One CEO we worked with turned over his entire staff two times and still insisted that he kept choosing the wrong people. How many lives need to be wrecked before people like this person get insight and get a little coaching themselves?

A NOTE FOR EXECUTIVES AND CEO'S

If you are at the top level of your organization, this is for you! There is nothing wrong with knowing ourselves and adjusting our own behaviors to help our organizations function more effectively. But many times that does not happen.

How would you like it if your 17-year-old son decided to take the family for a ride in the city in your new Lexus, blindfolded? As he started his journey with all of you in the car with him, he laughed, careening into poles and garbage cans, ignoring all of the family members yelling and telling him what to avoid, until, after the car is almost demolished, he turned to all of you in the back seat and said, "Now look what you made me do!"

As absurd as that is, some execs run their companies in just that manner. They get no feedback, or they are so unwelcoming that people are afraid to give feedback to them. They speak to no one, they make decisions without consulting anyone, or at least without thinking of the impact that the decision will make. And when morale is down and things start to fall apart, they blame the middle managers for their stupidity and ineptitude.

Instead of this type of dysfunctional behavior, how about a different climate? We experienced the opposite of this in an exec who held meetings around the clock to be there for people when they worked off shifts. He listened and served food on all three shifts. He took notes. Things they needed got changed. He knew as many people in the organization as he could. When he visited their workplace, and he did it often, he just stopped by to chat, and he would follow up on personal issues in their lives (Bill, how is that sick child of yours ... hope she is feeling better). People welcomed him when he came to their stations. His managers had training, and he attended all the sessions as a participant. When one struggled, he would ask us or others to coach them and help them get back on track.

When he had to have a wage freeze, he and his administrative team took a 5 percent reduction in their pay so the employees would know that he was suffering through it too. His management meetings consisted of 15 minutes of business and 45 minutes of discussions leading to decisions. He would call in anyone at any level to get feedback, but he never went around his middle management and encouraged people to use their problem-clearance or grievance process before going to him. He asked people to innovate, and instead of doing what many do (asking people to be creative and then punishing them and assigning blame if errors occur), he had the courage to let go of things that bombed and try new things out. He would move on and forget about it. He acknowledged people in public for successes and reprimanded in private. People felt safe to tell him when he was wrong or off track. He'd argue, but he would listen. When he moved higher in the corporate structure, to a corporate executive level, people cried. They should have. They knew he was the exception instead of the rule.

What do your people think of you? You are probably dominant if you have risen to the position you are in. You have power. How do you use the power? Are you respectful of those who don't have that power in the organization? How many of your cabinet have you fired? Why? Could any of their failures be attributed to you or your policies? How do you get along with your assistant executives? Do they function well as a team, or are they back-stabbing and cutthroat, attempting to save their jobs and position themselves in your favors. When is the last time someone told you off? What did you do to the person? Did you fire them? Did you have someone else fire them?

How are things going at your company? Do you have unions? And if so, is it a collaborative or competitive environment with them? How do you feel about your middle managers? Are they not accountable enough? Do they just not seem to get it? Do you sometime lament about the number of incompetent or disloyal people you have working for you? And do you admit to one thing only–you can't always pick 'em well?

When was the last time you wandered around just to chat with people? Do you know the names of at least 20 percent of your non-management staff? Would you feel comfortable letting them come in your office to exchange ideas, even if they are not articulate?

The CEO mentioned above would be with dignitaries and would stop to say hello to the housekeeping lady. Would you? Or would you make the person seem embarrassed about being "only" a housekeeper?

These questions seem trivial to some; after all, you have important things to do, much more important than wasting time on this touchy-feely stuff, they would say. But not many people at that organization mentioned earlier needed coaching. They modeled their leader. When there was a storm, they looked to see who was at the helm, and it was their leader–a person they truly respected, even when the decisions were not always good ones.

Like the old adage, "physician, heal thyself", we might say, "executive, coach thyself." It is of critical importance for your organization that you attend and participant in events like training and coaching with them. If you listen, use ideas, give credit, encourage, support and are AN EXAMPLE, you will be successful.

I saw an NFL referee say in a playoff game, "I don't know whether or not this is a review-able call, so I will check and let you know." What guts! What honesty! Even the announcers said, "Boy, you have to admire that. He admitted he didn't know. If only we had more refs like that." He put his ego aside to do what was best for the teams. What do we do? We need to be accountable to our people, as well as expect them to be accountable to us. We need to remember the four basic needs of trust, honesty, communication and respect. Don't be afraid to get some coaching from trusted outsiders, as well. You can't always speak to employees, even at trusted administrative levels, because at some point, they report to you. They will not be totally honest, unless you encourage that and are not vindictive.

You can't fly a plane without gauges. You need someone to be a gauge, a barometer, to tell you how things are. Many do this and then do nothing about it. Don't just get the needs assessment; figure out how to implement the plan. Talk to others not in your field, and with a coach to help you. Enhance and develop your own interpersonal skills. The executives who are most successful do that.

Don't be like that terrible boss in the old joke who dies. At the funeral, the preacher asks for a nice word from anyone to send the man's soul off in style. No one says a thing. Getting uncomfortable, the preacher clears his throat and asks again. Nothing. Finally, he says, "Certainly someone has something nice to say about him." A voice popped up from the back of the room and said, "Well, the guy before him was worse!" What do you want written on your tombstone? Hopefully it isn't *"Cranky and egotistical,"* or *"No one was worse."* Let's work towards establishing a climate where people do well, not because they work harder than anyone or they have some special skills, but because they model their leader.

We all want the client to apply the skills learned in the session. We want different outcomes. We want the person to act differently. And we do have a right to ask for that from the coach and the client. Part of how that happens is a change in perceptions on the part of both the client and the exec or manager. If the manager or exec has a perceptual mindset to see only the negative the person does, no matter how hard the client tries, she or he will not succeed, because the negative perception will become self fulfilling.

If managers are too starry-eyed and see only the good, they will not help the client change the inappropriate behaviors. We need balance. Use the code of conduct and action plan and get feedback from more than one person to see that the behaviors are changing; ask the coach too.

Clients also must change their perceptions. If their mindset is, "No matter what I do, I've been taken to the woodshed and I'm doomed here," they will sabotage themselves. You only do as well as you think you can. That is why we want people to be very careful of using labels. Once you are a_____, it is tough to see it otherwise. Remember the "8-mile minute" example from chapter three, in which the runner slowed his pace to avoid being quicker than he thought he really was? He didn't do it consciously; it just happened. Be careful of the self-fulfilling prophecy. What you expect you get.

We said before, corporate culture is shared perceptions. Much work needs to be done in an organization to change the shared perceptions. If the people are convinced that the top management doesn't know what they are doing, and are against the employees, you will have unrest, low morale and increases in grievances. If you would give an across-the-board increase, the people would say, "How much did they keep for themselves?" or "4 percent... we must be 6 percent underpaid....they still cheated us out of 2 percent."

Unless the perceptions change, all events will be filtered through that way of thinking, and nothing will improve. As Dr. Weisinger says, match the perceptions people have of you to the perceptions you have of them. Communicate, coach, model the behaviors you want, forgive, encourage creativity, mediate and problem-solve, hold people accountable (yes, we need to do that too) and be accountable yourself. Remember, you can't communicate too much, respect people too much or have people with too much self-esteem.

CHAPTER TEN

Key Points to Consider:

- It makes good business sense to help key employees enhance or remediate their interpersonal skills.

- Coaching can play a key role in helping successful people be more successful.

- Coaching can be used as an alternative to disciplinary action or termination.

Harnessing The Power of Conflict

CHAPTER ELEVEN

THE ROLE OF MANAGEMENT, THE BOARD AND OTHERS IN AUTHORITY

What role does the board, management or other administrative staff play in developing, supporting and encouraging self-mediated work teams? Here are some pointers:

The board should allow the leadership of the institution to do what it pays them to do–lead. If people from the team attempt to skip levels of authority and contact the board or other members of a higher authority, leadership who is contacted does a disservice by enabling the behavior to continue if they sympathize and take action. There is a real temptation to do this. If things are not going well, board members or authorities may feel that it is up to them to rescue the company or unit by taking charge, giving orders or assigning blame.

As we said previously, this may make leadership feel good, as if they are handling the problem; but it actually makes matters worse. The staff needs to be directed back to the person with whom they have a problem. They need to be asked to deal with the problem, personally, first. If this doesn't work, they can be encouraged to go up to the next level of management. Then, if all else fails, they can be encouraged to come back to the board, accompanied by the person or group causing the difficulty.

At this point, the board can help mediate a solution. If the board sets itself up as judge, however, it is likely the solution will not last. Remember, judge decreed solutions are not adhered to as well as mediated solutions, because in mediated solutions, people have a stake in making them succeed. The solutions are their solutions. They are not handed down to them from above. Also, mediated solutions create winners and winners, not winners and losers like the judge creates when she decides right from wrong. In judicial cases, the loser (the person judged to be wrong) naturally will harbor resentment.

How long will these kinds of forced solutions last? What happens when the board member or authority figure is no longer there? Usually in anger, the two parties resort back to the same old behaviors–behaviors that attempt to prove that one is right and the other wrong.

The best thing board and upper-level management can do is support the process, send staff with concerns back to those with whom they have an issue and honor the group's codes of conduct. If the staff ends up bringing issues back in front of a board, board members should act as mediators and not as judges.

Remember, leadership needs to look for common or shared interests in the role of mediator. As you listen to both sides, look for what both of the people need, and then make statements such as "It sounds like you both are looking for_____." Let your staff work out their own issues.

If you have children at home who want dinner, you make them dinner. As they get to their teen years, you teach them how to make dinner for themselves or for the family. You support the process. You may have special nights when they are responsible for the meal. If they complain, you don't immediately get up and say, "Fine, I'll do it." Instead say, "I can appreciate you not wanting to make dinner. Sometimes we don't like making dinner either, but it is your night. What do you think?" To just do it yourself teaches your children to be dependent on you. To encourage your children to do it themselves teaches them to be dependent on themselves. You may even look for shared interests. "Well, we are all hungry and we all want quick food tonigt; maybe tonight we'll do it together ..." At any rate, whether you mediate a solution or use the leveling or constructive confrontation process to listen–but still ask them to make dinner–at least you do not make it for them.

In the same way, you cannot make people get along. You cannot do it for them. You have to help them to get along on their own.

One client we dealt with had an administrative team that turned around a bad situation, changed some of its own destructive behaviors towards the team and saw the team mediate a phenomenal code of conduct. Not everyone bought into it, of course, and so eventually someone went to the board with a complaint. The board member should have said, "I really need to honor your code of conduct ... would you please take that back to your leadership and, if they don't help you resolve it, I will meet with you and your leadership to mediate an agreement." Instead, the board member listened and agreed and, without hearing all sides, chided the leadership for mishandling the situation. With that behavior, the board member began to destroy the positive process that the team built.

One thing that people need to understand is that not everyone wants to be empowered. Even though they profess the desire to be, many groups we have worked with have a difficult time with empowerment. Sometimes, they must take responsibility for things management used to be responsible for. They cannot complain anymore if they've truly been empowered. They can't let the other person do it. It is so much easier to put things back to the old way and blame others for problems. But if they can't blame others or go back to the ineffective way of handling things, these people will eventually change, stop causing problems and stay, or leave. However, if leadership enables them to continue old ineffective behaviors, they have only themselves to blame when the solutions do not work.

In another group, the CEO was instructed by the personnel manager not to listen to people who would come to the office and complain to him. Sure enough, people came in and he sent them back to the team, a behavior he had not been known to engage in the past. People complained for a while; but now the firm has teams that are functioning so well, they're engaged in progressive self-discipline and self-interviewing processes. A manager's observation was, "They handle so many things themselves, I have plenty of time on my hands to plan, sell and support company goals."

Supervisors, managers and administrators must be comfortable with the system and the process. They must be committed to the changes that will take place. In one organization, the leadership only half-heartedly agreed to the process, and then didn't accept the suggestions we gave to them. (Remember, the team's issues are perceptions and may not necessarily be real, but if they are real for the team, they must be dealt with.) When the administrator got in front of his team, he literally yelled at them for saying negative things about him. Instead of creating a solid work unit through the mediation process, he has raised anger and mistrust to higher levels than ever.

Beware of what you do when you use the techniques mentioned in this book in a work group. In reality you are creating a whole new culture. (A culture based on mutual respect as well as team goal achievements. A culture with openness and honesty, and with less back-stabbing. Less game playing. Less hostility.) The new culture will focus on improved relationships and solving problems at a lower level.

It will not be perfect. Like anything, there will be problems. It's OK to have relapses to old behaviors, but team members need to be gently reminded to adhere to the code of conduct and action steps. Renegotiate them if necessary. Write new action steps if needed. Do anything to keep interest in the process. Let it become the guiding policy on how to interact with others.

Even if it improves things just a little, wouldn't that be better than no progress at all? But do none of this if you can't handle the constructive feedback you're likely to hear or if you don't want the change in culture. It's better to have never done it than to profess a belief in an empowered group and not support the process. Before you start, we recommend you make sure you want a culture as described here.

But be warned: If you decide you want it the old way, it may be changed anyway.

What leadership should not do is to step in and problem-solve, express anger at honest feedback and constructive criticism or profess to believe in the process but act in the same old manner. What the leaders should do is support the process, help mediate solutions to problems, continually encourage the team and check on their progress, ask them to adhere to the code of conduct, check on progress with the action plan, and encourage members who are not adhering to the process to make decisions on what they need to do–while always being available to teach and support them if they wish to change.

Occasionally some people will need professional help. In a team we mediated, three people took advantage of references to individual counseling services. It sometimes happens that when a person no longer can function in a negative way on the team, a deeper pathology comes to the surface. Be ready to suggest that people seek assistance in a way that is both legal and helpful. An employee assistance program may be of value in these cases.

Parents should also support the mediation process with children. In the same way that a manager or board member should support staff employees and yet insist they try to work out issues on their own, so should parents respond to their children. Ask the children to work out issues on their own first–after teaching how to do so–and then mediate the problem with them if they can't. Remember, you have many options if mediation doesn't work. You can exert authority, use diplomacy, compromise or appease. If two children are quarrelling, sometimes a parent might support self mediation by saying, "Work out the issue between you or with me, or I'll decide for you; and you may not like my decision."

Whether at work or at home, mediation, leveling and coaching changes groups for the better, if those in authority allow the changes to take place.

CHAPTER ELEVEN

Key Points to Consider:

- Board and management should:

   Support the process;

   Redirect the the people;

   Mediate problems rather than decide for people.

Harnessing The Power of Conflict

CHAPTER TWELVE

HELPFUL TIPS FOR
MANAGING CONFLICT

CONFLICT RESOLUTION TIPS

Before you can be understood, you must first seek to understand: Let the other party speak first and truly try to understand, though not necessarily agree, with them. Then you can give your side. If you confront someone and they react, allow them to talk until they are finished before you continue. Ask questions to ensure they get it all out. Then they will be more receptive to hear what you have to say.

The majority of communication happens in the context of an ongoing relationship: Always keep in mind that preserving the relationship is equally important to getting your point across. Demonstrate your concern for the relationship by listening, asking questions and trying to problem-solve. Don't treat the communication process as a contest. If you win at the other party's expense, you damage the relationship.

The quality of the product or service delivered is dependent on the quality of the working relationship; and the quality of the working relationship is dependent on the quality of the communication: In business, if you want the highest quality product or service, you had better make your internal communication the best it can be. *People are not born communicators.* They need to be taught. Change and conflict can break down communication or cause it to be destructive. Invest in communication skills, and it will be reflected in the bottom line.

Rather than dealing with positions, look for the needs that the position is meeting: Don't immediately counter or react negatively to the other's position. Wait.

Remember positions are end products. They are the things that the other party feels will meet their needs. Once you can identify the other party's needs, then you can create multiple positions that meet those needs and yours.

Rather than focusing on feelings and behavior, focus on perceptions: Feelings and behavior are side effects. They are by products of perceptions. If you focus only on feelings and behavior, you have to guess at the reasons why other people are feeling and acting the way they are. More times than not, you will assume incorrectly and respond to them inappropriately. To truly understand someone, you need to understand how they see it.

Funnel up, not down: Most businesses and families try to problem-solve by reducing their options to two and picking one over the other. This creates winners and losers and damages the quality of the relationships. Why would you want only a couple of possible solutions to a problem? Creating multiple options to solve problems (funneling up) is the best way to go. Do not "boil it down to two and pick" or employ either/or thinking. When we create multiple options, we can find new solutions-usually ones that no one thought of initially-that meet most of the parties' needs.

Practice, practice, practice: Trying new skills is not easy. Most of us have had years and years to form our habits of confronting people and problem solving. It may not take years to learn new ways, but it does take time. And it takes practice to be good at anything. It takes practice, especially in these areas where emotions can be very intense and there is a lot at stake. Rehearse the confrontation or problem solving method with a friend or colleague. That's a much better time to make a mistake.

Silence is golden: Silence has a tendency to make people uncomfortable. Be able to look at the other party and handle the tension silence can cause. Some will say anything to break the tension of silence. Rather than react poorly, do or say nothing, especially if the other party is getting positional or argumentative. Silence has a tendency to make the other party a little uncomfortable and shifts the responsibility for keeping the conversation going to them.

Begin with a common ground, not differences: It is natural to start with our differences, because our differences cause our problems. Rather, look for common ground and say "yes" as many times as possible as well as asking questions that elicit yes's from the other party. Use statements such as, "I'm glad we could both agree to mediate," "Seems like we all want to solve our differences in different ways" or "Yes, you have a point." Reflecting back what someone just said will elicit a "Yes, that's right" response.

Attack the problem, not the person: Verbally attacking the other party only increases their defensiveness and escalates their emotions. Even if you feel that they are attacking you, don't retaliate. It serves no purpose in problem solving to lower yourself to critiquing personalities. Separating the person from the problem allows you to concentrate on solving the problem, not on personalities. Whether or not you like the other party, problem solving is not a game to see who can get the best of the other.

Be open to persuasion: Don't go into any meeting or enter into any problem-solving event without the ability to learn from the others involved. A closed mind or righteous attitude will doom any negotiations. In any interaction, be receptive to the other party's views and be willing to be persuaded. Being willing to be persuaded can be contagious. When you demonstrate your open-mindedness, others will likely follow. Sometimes it is better to open your mind and shut your mouth!

As Gandhi said, "An eye for an eye and everyone goes blind:" Don't lower yourself to the other party's tactics if they become demeaning. Continue trying to develop mutually beneficial solutions. Fisher and Brown (1992) in their book, *Getting Together,* describe an unconditionally constructive strategy as "doing only those things that are both good for the relationship and good for us, whether they reciprocate or not." For example, ask for the other party's input even if they don't ask you. If they are acting emotionally, you try to balance emotions with reason. If they misunderstand you, try to understand them. Even if they are not listening, consult them before deciding on matters that affect them.

Mirror their style: It is important to show respect in any problem-solving situation. If there are different cultures, cultural styles also need to be respected. One way to show respect and thus nonverbally communicate respect for the other party is to accommodate or mirror their style. If they speak slowly, do the same. If they are formal, be formal. If they take time to pause and reflect, you do likewise. This is called pacing, and it helps people feel empathy with you and your needs.

Remain optimistic: No matter what happens, communicate your optimism. Make comments such as, "Well, we both seem to have some strong feelings, but if we keep at it, I'm sure we can work something out" or "I can understand that you feel frustrated; I do as well. Let's review our needs and see what we have in common." Don't give up; you never know when something positive will happen.

Listening will solve 50 percent of the problems: Most people just need to be heard and acknowledged without someone jumping in and telling them what to do. Listening benefits more than the listener; it allows the speaker an opportunity to hear his or her own perceptions, as well. Besides, you just might be persuaded if you truly listen to the other side.

Mediate, don't litigate: Throughout most of our lives we have looked to parents, teachers, supervisors and the courts to make decisions for us. But if we can solve our own problems, we can be empowered by the experience. In any business or family, if problems can be solved at the level of necessity, others do not have to get involved. If you mediate, you retain some control and influence. If you let someone else make the decision for you, you have little control. While going to court or some higher authority may be appropriate at times, think of it as a last resort. Try to mediate; you have little or nothing to lose. Remember, to kill a fly you need a flyswatter, not an AK-47.

The process is equally important, if not more so, than the outcome: What we decide to do differently may or may not be effective, but if we negotiate based on needs, we can always come back to the table because the relationship is preserved. Preserving the relationship is a primary goal, as well as reaching an agreement.

Future versus past orientation: When emotions run high, we have a tendency to look to the past to either justify our position or point out the inadequacy of the other party. This neither helps to form an agreement nor to preserve the relationship. At times it may be helpful to cite examples from the past, but dwelling on history will just escalate the other party's emotions. We can argue what's happened in the past and who has done what to whom, or we can problem-solve about how we want to be different in the future.

How important is it? Ask yourself this question. If you answer it honestly, 8 times out of 10 you'll conclude it isn't that important. One colloquial participant told us, "Pick the mountain you want to die on," meaning that every hill (issue) is not worth fighting over. Decide what is important and what is not. If it's not important, Let It Go. You'll live longer. If you decide the issue falls into the 20 percent you must deal with, then try to solve the problem.

Turn negative statements into needs: Never defend yourself against negative statements. Instead, simply reflect them back in terms of how you perceive the other party's needs. If your child says, "You don't spend enough time with me; you're always working," respond with, "So you need us to spend more time together?" Do not say, "I do the best I can; besides, we spend more time together than most families." When you turn negative statements into needs, the other party feels acknowledged, which may be enough. If it is not enough, you can proceed to the needs-based problem-solving method.

Start with the easiest thing first: If there are multiple issues or problems to deal with, go with the smallest, easiest issue. Start with the least important issue in order to build some positive momentum before tackling harder issues. We have a tendency to want to start with the most glaring or emotionally charged issue. Resist this tendency, as it can put an initially negative spin on the whole problem-solving process.

Always leave the door open: If the problem solving or negotiation is getting stuck or you are starting to lose it, don't say, "This is getting us nowhere. I don't think this is solvable." Rather, say, "Well, I'd hoped we could have worked this out. We still have two days before the deadline. I would be receptive to another meeting. Please give me a call." A lot of agreements are reached in the 11th hour. If you shut the door because you get angry, you could blow an opportunity to reach an agreement.

Don't threaten, but warn of natural consequences: A threat is a promise of negative consequences usually imposed by you. A warning is a glimpse into the future of what may happen. Don't say, "Unless you get your grades up you'll be grounded for life." Instead try, "If your grades don't improve, your choices of colleges might not be that great." At work, save your threats to go to the boss as a last resort. Instead try to explain the potential impact on the company if things do not get done: "We need to get the diversity training implemented as soon as possible, because we don't want the employees feeling like we don't care!"

When confronting, start with "I" or "We" messages: When we think of confrontation, we think of telling others off or letting them know that their behavior impacts us in some negative way. Typically we start the confrontation with a "You" message. It may sound like, "You are too darned easy on the kids; they get away with murder around here." A "You" message used at the beginning of the confrontation only makes the other party more defensive and emotional. In order to assertively communicate your needs, state them in terms of "I" messages. Try saying, "I'm uncomfortable with the kids not realizing there are consequences for certain behaviors" or "We need to have a consistent approach to dealing with the children." While the other party may still get defensive or emotional, the intensity will not be as great.

When being confronted, start with You messages to get past the feelings and into the other's perceptions: When confronted, you need to fight the natural tendency to blame, defend, rationalize, minimize or explain. Your first step needs to be one of discovery. You need to find out why they are confronting you. And you need to eliminate the associated feelings of anger and defensiveness. If someone angrily confronts you, reflect it back with a You message. This will help you find out why they are angry so you can begin to remove the anger. If a peer at work were to say sarcastically, "Thanks for nothing," try responding, "You seem to feel that I've let you down?" Then they will tell you why they are upset with you. You can do something about the problem if you know where they are coming from. Once you find out why they are angry, you have multiple options to problem-solve.

Ask open-ended questions: In any problem-solving event, dialog among parties is important for many reasons. It allows venting, expression of needs, creatively developing solutions and the ability to listen and be heard while enhancing relationships. We need to ask questions that encourage or promote this type of dialog. Phrase questions to begin with "what, when, where or how" to encourage dialog. Do not ask questions that can be answered with a "yes" or "no." Avoid asking questions that begin with "why." "Why" questions tend to get positional answers.

Consider objective criteria: Another strategy in problem solving is to look to various sources for information or ideas. Sometimes this is a neutral strategy in that we are not picking one party's idea over another. We're agreeing on finding a third party to help. Suggesting that an expert opinion be sought is one way to offer a neutral strategy. Benchmarking with other companies or groups is another neutral strategy if problem solving bogs down. If you differ with your real estate agent over the asking price for your home, you may think you only have three options: You can stick with your asking price, accept the realtor's price or split the difference. However, with these choices, it won't be possible for both parties to feel their needs are getting met. Either just one party got their way or both got only part of what they thought was fair. If both parties could agree to get two appraisals and take the average, everyone wins. No one loses or feels cheated.

Offer choices, rather than asking for acceptance or rejection of your proposal: Try to avoid saying, "Take it or leave it," "Should we or shouldn't we" or "Can I or can't I." This forces the other party into an either/or proposition. It is better for all concerned to be able to select from multiple options to meet the needs of all parties. It is the shrewd 16-year old who, rather than ask mom if he can use the car to go to the movies, says, "Mom, I want to use the car to go to the show. Would it be more convenient for you if I went to the 6 o'clock or 8 o'clock showing?"

Invite criticism: Most people do not like criticism. But, in problem solving you need to invite it. Criticism gives you clues about the needs of the other party. Don't be afraid to ask the other party, "What is it about this solution that doesn't seem to meet your needs?" Inviting criticism also allows the other party to vent their frustration, which in turn should make them easier to deal with.

If the other party appears to be inconsistent or trying to deceive you, use the "Colombo" method: Only as a last resort should you accuse another party of trying to deceive you. If you are not sure, it's best to first try an indirect method to probe for information. The Colombo method is patterned after the TV detective series. The detective, sensing something was amiss in the witness' statement, would start out with questions like, "Could you help me understand ..." or "Maybe I'm missing something here; could you explain how ... ." The other party always offers more information to a nonthreatening question.

Don't commit too soon in the problem-solving process: Even if you are sure that your position is the only position that is workable, don't propose it or bring it up until the end, or near the end, of the problem solving process. Keep an open mind as you listen to the other side. Enter any problem-solving activity with the ability to be persuaded. If you commit too early to a position, it forces the other party into an either/or (your way or no way) proposition and halts the process.

If the other party commits too early in the process, help them back down with dignity: Since most people are not familiar with problem-solving techniques, they may make the error of committing too early in the process. Some think that playing hardball is a positive strategy, and they tell you that this is their final proposal and may threaten some consequence if you don't take it. When this happens, do not react to their position, but allow them room to back down with dignity. This helps preserve the relationship. If the union negotiator says, "This is our final offer-take it or we'll strike," you say, "I'm sure that's one option, but let's see if there might be another way to avoid that option and meet your needs."

Don't argue over whether something is a problem or not: Arguing the importance of an issue is rarely productive. In an ongoing relationship, if one party has a problem, all parties have that problem. While their issue may not seem that important to you, if they raised it, treat it as an issue worthy of your consideration. If your 5-year-old thinks there is a ghost in the closet and won't go to sleep, you can argue that there are no such things as ghosts, or you can discuss options for ghost removal like "shooing" the ghost out the window. In which scenario will the child sleep better?

Confrontation is the best way to nurture an ongoing relationship: Using the leveling or confrontation process, we confront perceptions, not feelings and behavior. By doing so, we do not allow other people's feelings and behavior to adversely affect us. If we care enough about others, we need to be able to tell them how they impact us and others around them. If we don't tell them, we enable them to continue to behave in ways that may not be in their best interests. As parents, sometimes we need to get on our kids because of their poor behavior. We do this because we love and care about them and want them to be good people. If done appropriately, confrontation strengthens relationships.

Reflective listening is foolproof; you can't screw it up. To demonstrate that you are listening, or to get emotions out of the way, verbally mirror the feelings you heard the person say. If you are wrong, they will simply correct you. For example, if someone were to say, "I can't believe you did that to me," and you respond, "You're feeling good about our relationship?" they'd probably reply, "Good? I'm incensed that you would treat me this way!" They will just correct you if you are wrong.

Accept responsibility for your own feelings and behavior: Most people are guilty of saying, "You make me so angry," "You are driving me crazy" or "You make me feel worthless." Remember what Eleanor Roosevelt said: "No one can make you feel inferior without your permission." Keep in mind that no one can make you do or feel anything you don't choose to. You control your own feelings and behavior. Once you accept that you are in control, you are empowered to feel and behave as you deem appropriate–not simply in reaction to others.

Crisis is opportunity: Few people change unless there is a jolt or crisis. The trouble is, if we handle crises poorly, we'll get the same poor results crisis after crisis. Each crisis needs to be approached (perceived) as an opportunity to do things differently–maybe better-and should not be dreaded and avoided. Every crisis is truly an opportunity to solve problems in a way that potentially enhances the relationship, not damages it.

Collect "yes's" (Ury, 1993): In his book *Getting Past No*, William Ury suggests that if you're trying to help parties in dispute resolution, ask questions all parties can agree on. Such questions would be, "Seems like these issues are very important to everyone concerned," "While we might not agree on the cause of the problems, sounds like you agree on the adverse effects the problems are causing," "Both of you are after a fair and equitable settlement," or "It would appear that we all think allowances are a good idea; we just need to determine how much." This helps set a positive tone for the process and demonstrates that the parties are not as far apart as they think.

Although it takes two to have a relationship, it takes only one to change its quality (Fisher and Brown, 1992): How we act to others often determines how they will react to us. If we don't like how someone is treating us, we have two choices. The first is to attempt to make the other person change. This is very difficult, especially if they don't want to change. The other choice is to change how we are acting. Often when we change the way we approach the other person, the other person will respond in a like manner. Let's say you are frustrated because every time you approach your spouse to discuss something, your spouse gets quiet. You might try to change how and when you approach your spouse. Perhaps a different approach will change the reaction you are getting. Since we have the most control over ourselves, we must start by changing ourselves first. Remember, it doesn't take much to impact a relationship. When a subtle change is made by one of the parties, things have to change.

If you blow it, accept responsibility and apologize: Apologizing is not an admission of guilt, but simply a statement that you own your responsibility for your behavior. Sometimes apologizing can help set the tone of the discussion so all concerned begin to examine their own feelings and behavior. Instead of blaming our behavior on others or rationalizing, defending or explaining ourselves, we also have the option to "own" our mistake, say we're sorry and move on. Rather than saying, "There's a good explanation of why I did it" or "That's not half as bad as what you do" or "Well, the reason that happened was ..." or "If you would just listen to me, I wouldn't have to yell," try saying, "I'm sorry I yelled. I guess I really felt the need to be heard, but I went about it in the wrong way." Apologizing is not for the weak. It takes strength to admit you are wrong and move on. But it can work wonders.

Pay attention to nonverbal communication: Ask for clarification if needed. Look for obvious nonverbals: scowling and crossing arms, not making eye contact, loud sighs, looking at watch or clock, shaking head "no" or silence. If you see any of these repeatedly, you should comment on the behaviors. But ask for clarification rather than accusing. Don't say, "You're mad and not listening!" Instead say something like, "It seems as though you are frustrated right now. Is that true?" Even if the person denies there is a problem, they will know that you are picking up on their frustration. Or maybe they haven't realized or admitted they really are angry.

Don't get snagged by barbed wire: Emotions can run high; when they do, be careful to not get snagged by barbed words or phrases such as, "You are never available," "You always talk behind my back," "You don't care at all," "All you care about is yourself," "You always side with Dad; don't you have a mind of your own?" "That's simply not fair!" or "I don't have to listen to you. You're not my real father anyway." Don't react, explain or defend yourself. Try to draw them to your side with statements such as, "It's important to you that I'm available," "Open communication is something we should probably look at," "Maybe we need to look at ways I can show you I do care," "While it may seem to you that I always go along with Dad, he and I agree on this issue and just want to find a solution we all can live with" or "I realize that I'm not your biological parent. We just need to find some middle ground here." This is difficult to do, but you need to resist being snagged.

When someone talks behind your back, confront them about the suspected behavior: Have you ever had someone tell you that another person is speaking ill of you behind your back? When that happens, confront the person you suspect of gossiping about you. Rather than attack, you may want to start out with an I message. You can say, "I need you to come to me if you have a problem with something I've said or done rather than going to others with it."

Or ask if what you heard is true: "I've heard you're not happy with the way I handled that incident the other day; is that correct?" In either case, even if the person you are confronting denies gossiping, they will know that somehow the word got back to you. This should make them a little more careful about gossiping in the future. If someone gossips to you, don't listen. As we have stated earlier, a wise woman once said, "If someone is gossiping too much, someone is listening too much."

If the person gets quiet and does NOT respond to you, use open-ended questions: Dr. Robert Bramson, in his famous book *Coping with Difficult People,* reminds us that when someone clams up, we should use open-ended questions, followed by a pause until we get the response we are looking for. Then we can encourage the person to continue to talk. You might say to a spouse who has gone silent, "Boy, I thought you'd have plenty to say about that topic; why are you so quiet?" Or you can say, "How are you feeling about what I just told you?" If you feel the other person is silent because they can't or won't make a decision, Bramson says to give them alternatives and deadlines. Show how making the decision will be safe for the person, i.e., it won't cause you or anyone else a problem. You might say, "We could go to the movie, go to dinner or rent a video. Since the movie starts at 8, we'll need to decide by 6 so I can ready. It's 5 now. I'll let you think about it until 6. I don't have a preference; we have the time and money to do any of the three."

Act consistently and ignore behaviors you do not want: Sometimes, inadvertently, we reward behaviors we don't want and ignore behaviors we want repeated. We reward the person who got all the work finished with more work to do. We get angry when someone does not do what we wanted; so we do the work ourselves or get someone else to do it. Bartz and Rasor, in their book *Surviving with Kids,* advise that we should ignore behaviors we don't want repeated and be consistent. Ignoring what we don't want repeated and being consistent can apply at work as well as in the home. At home, if a child asks one parent if he can do something and gets a "no," he may ask the other parent. The answer needs to be the same. At work, nothing changes–one supervisor should support the other, unless the other is wrong. If wrong, it should be left to the original supervisor to correct the error. For example, if Ted makes the wrong decision and his employee goes to Ted's supervisor, Mary, to ask her to reconsider Ted's decision, she should allow Ted to get back to the employee with a response rather than give the impression that she overruled Ted without him knowing it. Parents also can disagree in private but present a united front when possible.

If the parents want to have a family meeting to mediate an issue, but the children don't, the parents should ignore the complaining and simply state what time the meeting will begin and what the expectations are in regard to compliance. It is permissible to be forceful. Parents still have the right to make decisions, and not all decisions can be democratic. The same holds true at work. If the building catches on fire, we don't need group consensus to determine whether it's time to evacuate.

Harnessing The Power of Conflict

CHAPTER THIRTEEN

AN EXAMPLE OF THE
SELF MEDIATION PROCESS
IN A BUSINESS SETTING

It's a typical day at 5 o'clock, and Pat, a manager at QRS Corporation, is sitting in the office, reflecting back on the day. And what an interesting day it has been! The first thing that awaited Pat in the morning was a group of "representatives" from day shift who had mustered up enough courage to come in to complain about the fact that the night shift wasn't doing their share of the work. They couldn't be, accused the day-shifters, because every day, when they came in to work, the night shift had left a mess. No one could be that busy.

Pat sat and listened to one complaint after another:

"I don't get paid enough to clean up after them every day," said one person.

"I don't even clean up after my kids ... I'll be damned if I will clean up after co workers," said another, visibly angry. "I worked a rotating shift once, and they sit on their butts all night and take breaks. I hate to tell you this, Pat, but some people are thinking that maybe you don't say anything because either you're afraid of Shelly or because you hired Shelly and can't admit you made a mistake. Shelly is inept and doesn't do anything but moan and groan all shift. Shelly is the worst offender."

Pat squirmed in the chair and asked somewhat humbly, "Has anyone confronted Shelly on this? Or have you talked with anyone on nights about this matter?"

"Are you kidding?" Pat heard. "The last person who confronted Shelly quit in tears and spent a year in therapy to deal with it. I'm not going to get my face ripped off."

"Plus, we have to work with these people; we can't alienate them," another piped up.

"Besides, that's your job, Pat, not ours," a third muttered.

"It doesn't do any good anyway ... I tried that with PJ once, and it made matters worse; so I vowed from that day forward I will never confront any of them again," said a fourth.

"We came to ask your help, but like typical management, you put it all back on our shoulders. You confront them. You tell them that we're not putting up with coming in to this mess anymore."

They all left in a huff. Pat hadn't remembered when the group had been so emotionally charged. She figured it would be wise to check with the others on day shift to see if they shared these feelings. And she also knew the importance of checking with the boss, Fleman.

It wasn't exactly a joy to talk to Fleman. He had a habit of making a person feel like she would lose her job if something didn't happen. But he never had recommendations–just threats.

Pat finally got an appointment, which was always difficult. But after speaking with Fleman, she realized it had been a waste of time. In a Flemanesque manner, he snorted, "Get a handle on this, Pat. That's why you're paid the big bucks."

Returning to her office, Pat was too upset to start in on the daily To Do list. So it was nice timing when Terry came in to make things worse.

"I just wanted to let you know, Pat, that I was talking to Dana, who was honked off about not getting the vacation time requested," Terry began. "I think she wanted to punch you in the face. Apparently Dana has been planning that vacation for a while and had to cancel plans. When someone is that upset, I figured you'd want to know.

"By the way, I listened only as a co-worker and friend. Not that I agreed with her; I just want you to know I don't want to be in the middle of this."

"OK, thanks Terry," Pat said as she ushered her out. Pat decided to have lunch after her morning of turmoil, as if eating would help. When had it gotten so bad? Why didn't anyone seem to get along? Maybe it was because of the layoffs last spring. Or because of the reorganization that reduced the management team and made more work for everyone who was left. Maybe it was the introduction of the teams program. There was a lot of resistance to that. Some of the staff said it was just another fad to go through and that there was no such thing as true empowerment at QRS anyway.

Maybe it was the union campaign that failed two years ago. People didn't seem as fired up and happy about working anymore. Maybe the work ethic had changed.

Pat's lunch was neither delightful nor an escape from trouble. Eating alone, she overheard some people in the department talking. They had not seen her sitting behind the pillar.

"I wish Pat would quit. There's no control in the department anymore. Billie controls the department. No one says anything because Billie is explosive," said the woman with the egg salad.

"Billie sure gets away with murder. If I had that many absent days, I'd have been fired a long time ago. Not to mention the attitude ... like working with a living time bomb," a man continued.

"And there are so many cliques. I'm afraid of messing with some of those people. I really think if I told Pat about it, some of them would be waiting for me by my car. Then I'd be in trouble."

"I think poor Pat means well, but she wouldn't, or couldn't, do anything about it anyway."

All the different voices started to sound like the same person. They all began to speak in turn, one at a time.

"If I had enough money, I'd quit this place. I hate this place."

"Well, my spouse doesn't make enough for me to quit. I gotta have this job. I just do my work and go home. I try not to get involved with these people."

"I can't do that because I care."

"I care too, you know. I am just burned out from caring for a group of slime buckets that will stab you in the back the first chance they get."

"When I got reprimanded, Tony laughed at me. I doubt if I'll ever forgive him for that."

"You? What about when I ask Billie for help? All I get is grief. I figure, the hell with Billie, I'll do it myself. It isn't worth the pain of getting treated like crap for a week. It never used to be like this. You could ask for help and get it. You could eat lunch with anyone you wanted. People did their work and got along. I don't know what happened, but I feel the same way you do. I do my job, do the best I can and go home."

"My spouse is tired of hearing my complaints. But there's no one else to go to when you need to vent your feelings."

"Yeah, tell one of these people, and it's all over for you."

"God, I wouldn't think of telling anyone here, or Personnel ... or Pat."

Pat was devastated. That was the last straw. After lunch, she decided to call in those complainers and confront them. We'll get to the bottom of this once and for all, Pat thought.

As they entered, John asked Pat what was up. Pat got up and closed the door.

"I overheard a group of you talking at lunch, and quite frankly, I'm a little upset about it. Why didn't people come to me about these problems? You gossip and backstab and don't give me a chance to defend myself and that really honks me off! You don't think I'll do anything but you don't give me a chance. You're all a bunch of ingrates who only look at the bad side of things, and I'm sick of it!"

Pat was red in the face ... even before she was slapped with the next comment:

"Well, thanks for spying on us, Pat. You're an eavesdropper.

"I don't know what you overheard, but you shouldn't have been listening. We were just venting. And how dare you attack us just because you don't like hearing the truth. That's just like this place. I can't believe you've became one of QRS's Gestapo!"

Pat was both angry and apologetic. The group left in a huff only after she assured them that no discipline would take place against them. Pat was left feeling like she won but only because she was in charge.

No sooner did her disgruntled employees leave than Pat received a note that another person quit the p.m. shift. She got the message loud and clear that no one was willing to take up the slack, especially if QRS was too cheap to hire more help. The p.m. shift was already short one full-time and one part time employee.

Finally came the end of the day. Unfortunately, Pat realized it had been more typical than she would have liked. She wondered if it might be time to look elsewhere for work, but she really didn't want to leave. She didn't know what to do. As she packed up to go home, she remembered that the day before, Personnel reversed her decision to discipline after they had initially said they would support it. Three of her supervisors were problems, she thought. One is Attila the Hun, while another tries to be friends with everyone. The third seems to withdraw from issues.

Last month, Pat had brought in a motivational speaker, and for a couple days things did seem better. People enjoyed the speaker's humor and the program. But a month later, it seemed that no one had applied any of her good advice.

Pat also had called in an Employee Assistance Program (EAP) counselor to help. Although two people were referred for counseling, the suggestions by the counselor were largely ignored by her staff.

With an overwhelming number of problems facing her, Pat was concerned and bewildered. Taking a swig of antacid that she kept in the drawer, she went home. Later that week, Pat called in the Self Mediation Method consultants who were referred to her as a last resort. The consultants asked what the issues were, and as far as Pat knew, she enumerated them as follows:

1. Night shift isn't doing their share of the work. They continually leave a mess for day shift to clean up.

2. Shelly, a hostile-aggressive personality, does little work, and people feel that I don't do anything because I hired her.

3. People don't want to confront each other about problems. They feel it's my job to do all the confronting around here.

4. Fleman, the boss, won't support me in solving our problems.

5. Dana is mad about not getting vacation time granted, but Terry is the one who told me about it.

6. Layoffs and management reorganizations have created an atmosphere of mistrust.

7. A teams program (TQM) was initiated, but there has been tremendous resistance to it despite its objective of empowerment.

8. People feel Billie controls the department and that she's absent too much, but nothing is done because Billie is so explosive.

9. The department has become fragmented into adversarial cliques.

10. Tony's method, reprimanding people, hurt someone's feelings.

11. When I confronted staff about what I heard, they accused me of spying on them. I overheard the discussions at lunch.

12. The p.m. shift had someone else quit, and the staff is getting burned out on pitching in when we're short handed.

13. The supervisors don't help support the staff.

14. Personnel reversed my disciplinary decision, and I'm still mad about it.

"I don't know what to do now," Pat concluded. "That's why I called you two in. Can you solve these 14 issues? If so, I'll not only pay you, but I'll hug you both."

After a good laugh, the planning began. "We can help your people develop a framework for solving their own problems, Pat. First, we need to meet with the staff and see what they think. Sometimes they may interpret your reality a little differently than you do. Then we'll know what to do from there. But don't worry, Pat. It will get better ... probably after it gets a little worse."

Pat looked puzzled. "What do you mean, worse?"

The consultant smiled. "Your staff will have to get used to the new you and the new department rules. Some will probably struggle to bring the department back to its old ways, the way it was. But if you and your team members remain consistent, eventually these people will realize it's not going back to the way it was, and things will improve. If you or the team aren't consistent in this, though, you could have problems again."

"I feel like you just told me I can die or have major surgery," Pat grimaced. "But I guess if that is what needs to be done, let's have at it. It can't get any worse than it is. When should we have our first meeting?"

"That's up to you, Pat," the consultant replied. "You need to arrange it so everyone can attend. I'd recommend splitting up your shifts and having two sessions–one for one group and one for the other. It's even better if some members of each shift are there together.

"And Pat, you will have a separate feedback session on what went on, but you can't be part of this initial phase of mediation. If you were, people would either look to you for answers or clam up because the boss is in the room."

As much as Pat hated to admit it, she knew they were right. So Pat scheduled the sessions. As she talked it up among her staff members, Pat found that many of them were thrilled and hopeful they could finally get the department's problems solved. Pat hoped that the consultants would help them focus. This was, as one staff member put it, the last chance. They'd had too many false starts. This one had better work.

The first step that the group went through was issue identification. Here they outlined what they wanted more of, the same of and less of from each other and from management. The flip chart looked like this:

FROM EACH OTHER

MORE OF:
Sharing the work
Cleaning up after ourselves
Everyone being productive
Trust of each other
Communication
Ability to share negative concerns
The good sense of humor we used to have
The openness we sometimes have

SAME OF:
Loyalty to those in your own shift
Understanding with personal problems
Feeling a part of the things we do
Helping each other out
Friendships that we have established
Willingness to trade work times on the schedule

LESS OF:
Backbiting
Gossip and rumors
Cliques
Arguments between shifts
People who dominate and control by fear

On the question of what they want more of, the same of and less of *from management,* the group wrote the following:

FROM MANAGEMENT

MORE OF:

Support that we have been getting

Concern you show

Willingness to solve problems

Letting us run meetings

Follow-through on issues

Being available to staff for problem-solving

Taking charge and handling problem people

SAME OF:

Attempts at encouraging us to meet goals

Sense of humor

Concern at trying to make things right

Support for us to your boss

LESS OF:

Not dealing with jerks

Not confronting and expecting us to do it

Dealing with favorites different from the rest of us

Mistrust

New things like TQM without proper training for it

Letting cliques go on

Moodiness

Letting people hurt other people's feelings

Spying on us and more asking us what the problem is

Siding with supervisors when they are wrong

Letting Personnel make hard decisions for you

Letting shift-to-shift problems reoccur

After she read the list, Pat sat back. "Wow," she said. "I can't believe all the negatives for me. I know who said what. Some of these things have been brought up over and over again for a long time."

"All the more reason to hear and address them, Pat, without reprimand to your people," the consultant answered.

"I didn't mean I'd do that ... I just can't believe that some of these things are not settled. I thought they were over with."

"Again, as we told you before, whether they are real issues or merely perceived, you must acknowledge the issues in order for the staff to let go of their perceptions."

"Well, I guess I'm a little hurt right now. I thought they liked me."

"They do, Pat," the consultant responded. "They are just telling you what we asked them to tell you. Would you rather not know?"

"No, I guess I'm just going to have to take some time to get over the initial shock. Now what do I do?"

"Let us go through the rest of what happened, Pat; then we think you'll see what you need to do and what the group is going to do to improve things."

With that, the consultants began to show Pat the information in the summary report that they had prepared for her and the team. It seemed that things might improve after all.

The consultants began to teach the team how to mediate and resolve their own differences. The staff members all listened to the lecture on perceptions and constructive confrontation. They heard the information about mediation and participated in the practice exercises. They listed concerns and grouped them into areas of control and no control, and they clearly saw that they had a lot of control over how they communicate and confront each other and their supervisor, Pat. They understood the need to confront and knew that, despite personalities, if confronted by enough people over and over again, others would either begin to see problems to correct and would change or leave.

One woman on the p.m. shift liked what the consultant said about the process being like penicillin, not aspirin. The consultant mentioned that when you take an aspirin, your headache goes away. You only need to do it once. Penicillin must be taken over and over again; and if you take it all, over time, the illness goes away.

Once confronted, many people are likely to try to get things back to the way they were, when they had some control and they were comfortable. They may resist changing after one confrontation. They may even get worse. But if the confronting party remains consistent and continues to confront, eventually it gets better.

If you put your money in a pop machine and no pop comes out, you are likely to shake the machine. If the pop comes out when you shake the machine, you have just been taught to fight harder if you want to get your way. In a like manner, if you confront a person and his behavior gets worse so that you stop confronting, you have just taught the person that if he reacts badly, you'll cave in. Like penicillin, if you stop too soon, you get a bug that is really hard to kill.

The employees of QRS learned that they must be consistent and repetitive for this to work. And they had to agree to practice confrontation, use it and be willing to have it used on them. If they did, the place would get better. It always does when people are open and honest and truly listening before responding.

After the employees were trained, the leadership of the department (Pat) was also trained. Then, all were brought together at a follow-up session. Pat was instructed to tell her staff that the feedback was appreciated, that management would learn from it and that the staff members should do likewise.

The staff and Pat developed a code of conduct and action plan. The code of conduct looked like this:

QRS CORPORATION CODE OF CONDUCT

1. Check out perceptions with others before jumping to conclusions.
2. Do not listen to or participate in the rumor mill.
3. Bring issues to the person concerned first; if that doesn't work, bring them to Pat and have Pat *mediate* the issue with the two parties.
4. If someone violates the code, remind them gently to adhere to it.
5. Utilize leveling or confrontation and mediation. Use peer mediators if needed.

The employee action plan and the manager action plan looked like this:

STAFF ACTION PLAN, QRS CORPORATION

Issue	Action Steps
1. Sharing the workload	a. Take assignments without complaint.
	b. Rotate making out assignments.
	c. Each person gets one "easy" and one "difficult" assignment each week.
	d. Mediate concerns about workload.
2. Gossip/rumors	a. Refuse to participate in rumor mill.
	b. Confront individual who spreads rumors.
	c. Check out perceptions before acting on them.

MANAGEMENT ACTION PLAN, QRS CORPORATION

Issue	Action Steps
1. Support for staff	a. Give routine positive feedback.
	b Have meetings with each employee on regular basis.
	c. Do not cancel meetings once established.
	d. Support staff with superiors, if they are correct.
2. Not dealing with jerks	a. Use the progressive discipline process, if warranted.
	b. Tell people you are dealing with a problem, but do not tell what you are doing with whom.
	c. Mediate minor problems as they occur.

What eventually happened to our friend, Pat, and the QRS Corporation after going through the process? Let's look at a snapshot of the company now.

It's been a typical day. At 5 o'clock, Pat is sitting in the office, reflecting back on the day. And what an interesting day it has been! The peer mediation team, which was created to mediate differences between day and night shifts, had just presented Pat with their issues. The team listed the issues they have control over and their shared interests. They also wrote a code of conduct that includes the use of the leveling or confrontation process and an action plan with first steps on how they will attempt to solve their problems. Pat realized from their notes on "What we need from our manager" that she has some work to do as well. The main item that Pat will work on is responding to people in a timely manner and being honest when there is no answer instead of telling people what they want to hear to try to keep the peace.

Shelly tendered her resignation that afternoon with the comment, "Too many of these damned people have been confronting me about problems using that stupid leveling process, and I don't think I'm that bad. So I'm going to a place where I can do the job I was hired to do." Pat was all too happy to receive her resignation since Shelly had decided she didn't want to change.

Fleman is happy with Pat and with the team and has managed to stay out of their hair. That's fine with me, Pat thought. If Fleman stays out of it, my staff won't be enabled to continue poor behaviors.

Terry said that Dana was still angry with Pat, but Dana had used the leveling (confrontation) process, and Pat had listened, hoping that Dana's anger would subside in time. Pat encouraged Terry next time to tell Dana to go directly to Pat, rather than listening to Dana and violating the code of conduct.

Billie, the time bomb, had fizzled. Her attendance and attitude improved because Billie needs the job-and the team had confronted her about the favored status. Pat also has been careful not to favor Billie, time bomb or not. She recently told Billie that the work must be shared equally, since getting the job done and making the team successful is a shared interest. Billie agreed and has been trying.

Pat called in an Employee Assistance Program counselor to help deal with the residual feelings from the layoff. As a result of that meeting, two people made personal appointments with a counselor to deal with anger issues and other nonwork related problems.

The team program is going much better. Pat has a quality team looking over issues on how to make the department run better. The quality team has adopted a code of conduct that they use at each meeting. The team has decided how to do better work with less people. They proposed a gain sharing program to split the salary of people who left the organization. If the team can work productively without incurring overtime, and they meet company financial goals, they will all share in the savings. No one complains about being understaffed anymore. Some people still don't like Pat, but after an attempt to mediate problems between them, one decided that the department interests take precedence and that Pat was not a friend. Pat can live with that. "Not everyone will like me," Pat thought.

Tony was reprimanded for laughing at another employee who received disciplinary action. When Tony went to a higher authority, the authority listened and tried to take action. Pat is meeting with the authority tomorrow to discuss how they operate, to show the code of conduct and to ask the authority's cooperation in the future.

Personnel reverses few decisions now, because there are less decisions to reverse. Pat has thrown away the antacids. Now, she drinks mineral water. It isn't perfect, but it's a lot better than what it was, and Pat will go home tonight feeling like something was accomplished. It wasn't so bad of a day after all.

Harnessing The Power of Conflict

CHAPTER FOURTEEN

EXAMPLES OF THE SELF MEDIATION METHOD IN A FAMILY SETTING

Mark and Lois sat next to each other in the therapist's office. It was Lois' turn to speak. She didn't know sometimes if it was such a good idea to get married to Mark so quickly after her divorce from Jack.

"I had known Mark for years, and he seemed to be just what I was looking for," she began. "Whereas Jack was impaired, Mark didn't drink or do drugs. Jack had been stubborn, and he was cold and aloof with the children. Then, after he got into addiction recovery, he still didn't seem to pay much attention to any of them. Mark is so warm and loving, and he loves my children. Jeremy really looks up to Mark. Mark is the dad that Jack wasn't. He plays ball with him and goes places with him. He even let him come to the office and watch him at work. That was great for an 8-year-old.

"Heather likes Mark, but she is still a little distant, and she's into her `16 year-old thing.' When he tries to talk to her, she rolls her eyes and says, 'Whatever' in a preppy little voice. It makes Mark angry, but he keeps it under control. He usually tells me, `You do something ... she's your daughter.' "

Jane had been in private practice in marriage and family therapy for 17 years and had seen many families with similar issues. She had mediation training from the court system and from the seminar she had attended.

"Then there are Mark's kids," Lois continued. "He has them every other weekend and for three months during the summer. Marsha is 17 and goes to Heather's school. The problem is that they didn't like each other before we got married, and they really don't like each other now. Heather is cute, but not very athletic and slightly overweight. Marsha is a cheerleader, she was homecoming queen, and she plays soccer, cross country and track. She is tall, beautiful and very popular. She dates a lot and is a pretty well-adjusted girl, but she has her own friends who are in the `in-crowd.' Heather didn't go to homecoming. She's a sophomore, while Marsha's a junior. More and more, Marsha has been asking Mark if she can skip the visits because she has other things to do. One time, Heather overheard Marsha telling Mark that she, Heather, was a geek, and that Marsha hated coming over to babysit the brats. Mark didn't know that Heather heard it, but luckily, he stuck up for Heather. Heather heard that too, but her feelings were hurt and it put a bigger wedge between the two girls.

"Andy is 7, and he's a real hellion. I think he is hyperactive or something. I talked to Mark once about medication for him, but he wouldn't hear of it. Michael is 10, and he's mad at his father for divorcing his mother. He just sits on the stairs and reads while the rest of the family is in the kitchen. He's not ready to let me do things for him, or with him. It's difficult, especially when they're all here for three months. Michael gets along well with Jeremy–my son-but I think he's a little jealous of the time Jeremy gets to spend with Mark. Andy treats Jeremy just like an older brother; he bullies him and teases him constantly, and Jeremy falls right into it and tattles on him. Mark is really hard on Michael, but he just wants him to turn out OK, without medication.

"Then there's Peanut. Her real name is Angela, and she is a doll. She's 6 and acts like she's 16; she's so mature for her age. She just loves everyone on both sides of the family.

"This last Thanksgiving was a disaster. We were ready to sit down and eat. Marsha showed up late, but she pitched in and helped me cook and I was really shocked. She talked to me and told me about what she was doing at school, and how she had such a great time in track and that she was chosen for the all-conference team. She had never talked to me so much before. I just let her talk while I listened, and it felt so good. I started to believe she was accepting me. I didn't notice Heather sulking in the other room, glaring at us. Marsha and I were cracking up as if we were old college friends. Now, Heather seldom talks to me, and she NEVER cooks with me or does anything with me. She and I pretty much just fight. Mark says it's because she is trying to break away from me, but I think there's a lack of closeness because of the divorce and my remarriage.

"At any rate, I was so thrilled to actually be communicating with a teenager, that I didn't realize Heather was getting jealous and angry. That is, until she called Marsha a nasty name and stormed up to her room. Marsha just shook her head. She seemed so mature at that moment, and I just smiled and shrugged, and we went on talking. Mark was the one who went up to see if he could talk to Heather. Maybe I should've gone up, but I was so embarrassed by her acting like a 2-year-old that I figured the heck with her, let her sulk. She told Mark to get lost. So he left her alone and went back to playing with the boys.

"When it was time to carve the turkey, Marsha told me she couldn't stay for dinner. Mark was furious, but I think I understood. Mark told me later that he thinks she was just being nice to butter me up so I wouldn't be mad when she ducked out. If that was her plan, it worked. In front of everyone, I told her it was OK after Mark had said it wasn't. Right away, I could tell that upset him a lot. Marsha said she was going over to her boyfriend Todd's house, and then Mark said, `Marsha, this is a time for family to be together, not strangers.' So Marsha shoots back with, `Then why aren't we home with Mom, Dad?' Neither Mark nor I said anything. So then Marsha came up and gave me a big hug and said, `Thanks for being so cool, Lois. I didn't mean that to hurt you. I think you're OK, you know.' I told her I understood and asked her to come back with Todd after dinner for some pumpkin pie. She said she would and then rushed out of the house. There I was–Mark glaring at me, and Heather refusing to come out of her room.

"Andy, Michael and Jeremy got in an argument right then about who would help Mark carve the turkey. Andy grabbed the knife from Michael and told him, `Get lost twerp. If you touch this knife, you'll cut yourself ... not that I would mind.' So Michael called him a nerd, Andy called him a dweeb, Michael called him scum, and then Andy pushed Michael. Michael just went over to the stairs, and started in again reading his paperback. He didn't even cry. I think he just runs off anymore if it gets too rough.

"Jeremy tried to stick up for Michael, and Andy punched him in the arm so hard it left a mark. Mark got up to go after Andy, but I put a stop to it. Once again, I made Mark very angry; but at the time, he didn't say anything about it. He just glared at Andy and told him, `If you punch Jeremy or anyone else again, you'll spend a lot of time in your room, young man.' Then he made him apologize to Jeremy. This was a death warrant for Jeremy. As soon as Mark left the room, I could hear Andy making fun of him. I heard Jeremy tell him, `Shut up, creep.' Andy replied, `Oooooh, creep. Boy am I hurt by that.'

"And then there was Angela. She was supposed to clean up her toys. But she hadn't, and Mark slipped on one of her toys. He was so frustrated by that time, he didn't know what to do, so he yelled at her and she started crying. I was afraid to pick her up, because I didn't want to go against him again. Before I could decide whether or not to, he did, and pretty soon she was sleeping in her Dad's arms.

"After dinner, things calmed down. Andy tried to talk to Mark, but he was so angry, he told Andy he didn't want to discuss it. When Andy left, I heard him mumble, `What else is new?' under his breath. After the kids were in bed, and Marsha and her boyfriend had left, Mark and I finally got a chance to sit down and talk. I told him, `Mark, I think I screwed up today and made you mad. Am I right?' Mark was hesitant to speak about it at first, but then he admitted he was angry with me. He told me he barely has the kids enough to have any control anyway, and when I asserted myself, I made it worse by countering him. He said he loves me, but this is really frustrating. Well, I was frustrated too. I'm just trying to build a relationship with them, and it's been hard. I know he thinks Marsha was manipulating me, but I think she actually likes me. I can relate to her, and it means a lot to me. Heather can barely relate to me now.

"So anyway, Mark made the suggestion that we should go see the counselor that my friend Peggy went to, and that's how we ended up with you, Jane."

Jane sat back in her chair. That was quite a mouthful ...

"Well, it sounds like you both made a good decision to seek help," Jane finally said. She looked at Mark. "Mark, do you agree pretty much with Lois' assessment?" Jane asked.

"Entirely," he said. "We need to work out some of our issues so we can make this thing work. It's not easy with six kids who aren't exactly the Brady kids."

"Nor will it become the Brady Bunch," Jane laughed. " But I hear that you both want to handle these situations differently."

They all spoke for a while longer, and then Jane had both of them meet with her again. She already had had a sequence of meetings, met with each party individually, and had spoken to the children.

Jane began the second session, and Mark and Lois again were together. "I've written some notes down from the meetings we've had and I'd like to see if we can start to clarify some of our issues," she said. "Mark, your perception of Lois was that she sometimes interferes with your establishing control in the household. Often this is done to make her look good to your kids. You also perceive that she encroaches in your area when she keeps insisting that Andy be put on medication.

"Lois, you seem to feel that Mark loses his temper so infrequently with the kids that, when he does, you're afraid he'll become just like Jack, your ex husband. You said Jack was always harsh with everyone.

"You also think that Mark interferes with your ability to build relationships with the kids, especially Marsha, although you seem to recognize that sometimes you can be easier on Marsha than Heather.

"The kids feel confused. Some of them think that you are too wrapped up in your own lives to work out the issues you're facing. And, in general, they feel that you are somewhat unapproachable."

"I can't believe they'd say that about us," Mark interrupted.

"I know, Mark, but remember I told you this wasn't an easy process, there are no quick-fixes," Jane said. "In our meetings, we also talked about your needs and shared interests. I have a list of those I'd like to have you look over." She handed out the following list:

Shared Needs:

1. Mutual respect for each other and the right of each one to discipline the children.

2. Talking to each other before decisions are made.

3. Trust that people will be true to themselves.

4. Both adults and children need to be listened to and have opinions considered.

5. Need to have parents be approachable (kids too).

6. Need to allow relationships on both sides to develop.

7. Need to let each parent (and all kids) make mistakes.

After everyone agreed that this indeed represented a list of their shared needs, Jane scheduled another appointment to help them come up with a code of conduct and family contract.

When they were all together, Jane began the session. "We have lots of people in the office today, but you have all participated well, so we probably won't have to be here for more than an hour or so. First I want to look at what we have already accomplished on the code of conduct. Let me remind you that, as part of our group rules, we all agreed that we would let each other talk one at a time, without interruption; that we would not have side comments; and that we would pay attention to what was going on. OK, here is the code of conduct I heard you agree to."

CODE OF CONDUCT:

1. We'll allow ourselves time to get to know each other and develop as a family unit.

2. We respect each other, and don't hit each other or call names. We ask for what we want rather than act it out or take it out on others.

3. We are approachable with one another.

4. We express our anger directly.

5. Mom and Dad can talk privately before rendering a decision.

6. It's OK for the kids to be who they are.

Jane asked, "Is the code of conduct reflective of all your needs?"

Andy jumped in quickly, "Does that mean I can't goof around with my brothers anymore?"

"As long as you don't hit them or bully them, I think you still can have lots of fun with them," said Jane.

"Yeah, I think I can live with it," said Heather.

"Sounds OK to me," replied Marsha.

"What do we do now, Jane?" asked Mark.

"Well, at this point, I'd like to talk about developing a family contract where you can address issues that all of you identified and come up with some steps you could take to eliminate some of those issues. I'm going to ask the kids to step out for just a second while I talk to Mom and Dad here. Lois, let's start with you."

"Mark and I spoke about our need to be unified in our decision-making with the kids," Lois said.

"Let's call that issue decision-making," Jane said, as she wrote in her notebook. "Mark, what is one thing that can be done to aid in this process?"

"Well, I suppose we should check with each other before making decisions that affect us all," Mark said.

"I'd agree to that," Lois said.

"Anything else with this issue?" asked Jane.

"We need to make sure we are treating all the kids consistently and gently call it to each other's attention when we feel we aren't," Mark said.

"And I think we should allow for relationships to build with each other's kids as well as our own," said Lois.

Jane said, "Great ... anything else in this area? No? OK, let's go on to the next parent issue, which was having the time to relate to the children and deal with issues on an ongoing basis. Both of you expressed the need to set aside more time for this."

Lois said, "Let's set aside 15 minutes each week for each child. This would be uninterrupted time. Maybe we can meet in the afternoons, after school."

"I can't meet in the afternoons," said Mark.

"But do you agree that meeting is important, Mark?" Jane asked.

"Yes, I think that would be OK."

"Good. I'm not too concerned about the time; you two can work that out with the kids later on. The important thing is that you both set aside that time. Anything else?" Jane asked.

"Only one more that I see," Lois said. "I think we need to let our kids finish what they have to say in these meetings before we give our point of view."

"Sometimes you need to interrupt," said Mark.

Jane added, "That's true, Mark, but for the most part, can you agree to try to let them vent before you folks speak?"

"Sure, that would be fine."

"Good," Jane said. "Now what about the issue of consistency? When we talked, Lois, you mentioned that it was difficult to be consistent all the time, but we spoke about the importance of at least attempting to be consistent. You don't want to give special treatment to anyone."

"Yeah, we can agree on that," said Lois.

Jane then added, "Good. Let me bring the kids back in now." Jane invited the children back into her office and started the conversation. "Kids, you had two areas of concern. One was a concern about jealousy with one another and the second was bullying. Let's look at the jealousy issue first. Any thoughts on that?"

Marsha said, "Well, we've been talking about this, and we decided that the best thing to do is that each person worry about themself and not worry about what the other person is doing."

"...and that's probably just fine with all of us," said Heather. "We all have things we can be proud of, without having to be like someone else."

"That sounds like a good way of looking at it," Jane added. "Keep in mind, it isn't easy sometimes. It's kind of human nature to wish we could be like someone else, or to wish we could do things that others can. But we can talk later about some things that we can help you with if you're having any difficulty in that area. Now, what about the issue of bullying? Andy, how do you feel about that?"

"I always get blamed for everything," Andy snarled. "Michael does things that are bad, but I'm always getting in trouble. Sometimes he asks for it."

"Yeah, and I don't like getting punched all the time either," Michael said.

Jane jumped in quickly to direct the conversation. "Andy, can you figure out some other ways to deal with some of your frustrations, without hitting anybody?"

"Yeah, I guess I could. If that doesn't work ... I'll just get on my bike and ride for a while," Andy said.

"Good idea," Jane added. "You are all going to get the opportunity to meet with your Mom and Dad once a week to talk things over; I'm wondering if that would be a good time to talk about some of these issues with them?"

Jane continued, "We have one last issue to deal with. Angela sometimes has trouble remembering to pick up her toys. If she does, maybe she could receive points towards a new one? Or, here's another suggestion. Have you ever considered a 'toy jail?' If Angela doesn't pick her toys up, they go into a box that we call a toy jail. We leave the toy in the toy jail in plain view of her for a whole day. If she doesn't remember to pick up the toy after that, the next time it's in the toy jail for two days. Angela what do you think about that?"

"OK," said Angela.

Jane stood up. "I think you all have done some good work here. You should all be proud of the family contract you came up with."

The contract read as follows:

FAMILY CONTRACT

Parental Concerns:

1. Decision Making
   a. Check with each other before making decisions.
   b. Treat kids consistently.
   c. Allow for relationships to develop.

2. Approachability
   a. 15 minute meeting with each child each week.
   b. Let child vent uninterrupted, when possible.

3. Consistency
   a. No special treatment for anyone.

Children Concerns:

1. Jealousy
   a. Worry about ourselves and not the other.

2. Bullying
   a. Talk about concerns with parents.
   b. No hitting.
   c. Ride bike or use some other way to get out frustrations.

3. Picking Up Toys
   a. Toys not picked up go into toy jail.

"So, how are things going?" Jane asked at the next session.

"Great," said Lois, as Mark nodded his agreement. "It seems that Mark and I are being more consistent in our decision-making. And, we are also trying to consider the impact of our decisions on the whole family. Angela is picking up her toys. She's only had one toy in jail so far, and she's remembered ever since then. We gave her a reward for remembering.

"We are talking to all the kids about the things they have on their minds. I didn't realize how much Heather thought that I liked Marsha better than her. Heather and I also have been doing more together. I think Mark was trying to tell me that all along, but I needed to hear it from her before it sunk in.

"Andy has been riding his bike more frequently. I guess he's trying to deal with his stress without hitting the other boys. He's doing a little better, but Mark and I decided that he needs to continue seeing you for a while, Jane. He still seems so unhappy.

"I don't think Marsha and Heather will ever be best of friends, but at least they talk to each other at home, even if they still don't at school. I guess that would be too much to ask.

"All in all, I think the code and the family contract was a great idea. Now, I'm not dreading the arrival of summer like I was. We've got a great way to deal with our concerns."

Harnessing The Power of Conflict

CHAPTER FIFTEEN

PUTTING IT ALL TOGETHER

As you can see, the techniques of Harnesing the Power of Conflict are common sense, nuts and bolts ideas and concepts. Some of what you have read, you already knew. We just packaged it a little differently. Many fads of creating quality interpersonal relationships or cultural change have come and gone, with varying levels of success. But even common sense, as we quoted Steve Covey earlier, "is not common practice"–especially when relationships are highly conflicted or possess a heightened level of negative emotion. Common sense, then, usually goes right out the window, and we default to fight or flight. However, we can <u>change</u> that default, just like a computer, and be able to apply common sense concepts no matter what the issue.

It is the skilled executive, consultant, coach or parent who can assess a situation and prescribe the appropriate level of intervention. We have found through our experience that "less is more" is a good rule of thumb. Doing enough to help, but not doing for. Most work groups, executives or families experiencing difficulty just need a little help seeing where they are stuck and acquiring the skills to help them more forward; they can do the rest.

The techniques of *Harnessing the Power of Conflict*, 3rd Edition can be used singularly or in combination. When we first started working collaboratively in the early 1990s, our focus was on work groups. As we mentioned in the preface, we learned as we went and as good researchers do, we attempted to replicate our process with different groups. So we were applying all the techniques of Harnessing the Power of Conflict to diverse groups with good success. Our goal was twofold: to help the work group correct the current problems and to teach new skills so that the work group could self-correct in the future. Thus, we called our process the Five-Step Self-Mediation Method (TM). The Self-Mediation Method consisted of the following five steps:

Step One: Issue Identification

Step Two: Understanding Human Behavior

Step Three: Acquisition of Interpersonal Skills

Step Four: Code Of Conduct

Step Five: Action Planning With Follow-Up

As we continued using the Self-Mediation Method, we began to see that all groups did not need that level of intervention. Some groups were functioning adequately and just needed skill training (step three). Others needed new ways to communicate interpersonally through the organization (steps two, three and four) and did not have major cultural issues. Still others needed action planning and follow-up for the leadership (step five, which later evolved into coaching). Moreover, some smaller companies and organizations could not commit the time or afford the cost of such an intensive intervention.

After deciding to write this 3rd edition, we asked Ms. Jennifer Cox-Baker to write the forward, explaining her experience with our process. Upon reading her description of her experience with pieces of the Self-Mediation Method, it reinforced that indeed less *is* more. Her organization was responding to a need for skill training (not requiring the entire self-mediation process), and it had far-reaching results with just that piece.

So some or all of the techniques can be used, depending on the situation. Just as Blanchard's situational leadership model advocates for assessment of the situation and then using the appropriate leadership style to match the needs of leader and work team, we advocate an assessment of the team needs and then application of the appropriate principles we have discussed to meet those needs. Emotional intelligence, as we have mentioned, says that the most successful individual assesses the situation and uses the appropriate emotion to the degree necessary to solve the problem and enhance the relationship.

Although there is not a chart that equates a certain situation with a prescribed solution, like a doctor diagnosing a patient and then prescribing the exact treatment regimen in a scientific way, we do feel that we can offer suggestions on what the appropriate course of action may be if presented with a particular problem. Again, these are suggestions; because we are dealing with people, you may find that our suggestion may not be 100 percent effective in your situation. This is not an exact science. But these suggestions may help give you some ideas that you can try. If they do not work, and you have a working relationship, you can always try another one without damaging that relationship.

- If the group has some minor issues between individual members, but it is not widespread, you might use **leveling** to confront only those who have the issue.

- If the group has a leader, manager, executive or a unique professional–or if you are a board member who feels these techniques can be useful for someone in authority–you may want to try **coaching** that individual. If the actions of this individual have damaged the rapport of the group, the **Self-Mediation Method**™ may be appropriate.

- If the group is generally in good shape, but you see that the interpersonal skills or customer service skills are in need of strengthening, you may want to consider the **conflict management/mediation training pieces.**

- If the group has subcultures and pockets of dissent, and you feel that the problems are now the focus, your quality is suffering, or productivity is being compromised, then the **Self-Mediation Method**™ may be in order. You may even want to help train **peer mediators** in order to have someone whom people can go to for help who does not do their appraisals or have the power to fire them.

- If you want to have a motivational program to get people energized to work though difficult times, the conflict management speeches can be used in that manner. The information on **change, changing perceptions, leveling or mediation** can be individual programs and speeches, as well.

- If you are confused about the nature or extent of the issues, but you know there is unhappiness or unrest in the team, diagnostics can be performed or consultation may be of benefit. Then the appropriate course of action can be determined.

A number of support materials were developed to help assist trainers and consultants to use this material and to support them in acquiring the skills of mediation. Audio tapes, video tapes, and workbooks can be helpful in presenting this material to others and are available as part of this process to assist others in getting the word out.

The quality of the ongoing service or produce is in direct proportion to the quality of the ongoing relationship. If the relationships are compromised, your foundation is weakened. The techniques and processes in this book help fortify those foundations so you can get to the important work that you do in this world. We see how different businesses make unique contributions to the betterment of life for all on this planet. We are grateful for the opportunity to help those businesses accomplish what they were created to do, by helping the leadership and the team members feel comfortable, happy and productive as they go about the tasks they have chosen to do in this life.

It makes no sense to be miserable. There is no time for it. When you are miserable, you impact others, many others, and make them miserable too. Don't wait until problems get out of hand and someone must go. Intervene at the earliest possible time. If you do, you will strengthen groups and help them flourish. Good luck.

Harnessing The Power of Conflict

SURVEY INFORMATION ABOUT HARNESSING THE POWER OF CONFLICT

What Self Mediation Method participants are saying about the process:

A recent survey concluded that 65 percent of recent hires cited "open communication" as the most important factor for taking a new position. When communication breakdowns are addressed and this program is conducted for companies, improvement in workplace communication occurs. A random sample of participants were surveyed to see what changes occurred as a result of using *Harnessing the Power of Conflict*. The purpose was not to secure statistical information, but simply to gather a sampling of responses from participants in the process.

One manager commented:

"The atmosphere on the unit is totally different from when we did team building. The remaining staff are enjoying the new staff and remain very positive for the most part. Many of the pot-stirrers have moved on to other areas, some of whom are causing problems in those areas, also."

"I feel that this program helped refine skills needed to confront difficult people. Staff continued to feel uncomfortable confronting at times; however, they seemed more willing to discuss the issues and help resolve them. I feel that the experience was a positive one and have recommended it to other nurse managers. Thanks."

Here are some of the other comments from participants:

If you have attempted to use other programs or processes, how has this process compared to those? Why?

- Better than other programs. The way the program is presented encourages you. It eases tensions to use leveling confrontation and not be afraid to do so.

- Better than other programs. Simple, real life, easy to understand.

- Better than other programs. Quick and easy to use.

- Better than other programs. People don't feel like they are being accused or attacked.

Have you met your goals? How?

- Yes, by being more assertive, confronting problems as they happen instead of stockpiling them.

- Yes, communication is easier since I have learned how to handle the way I express my feelings.

- We did a good job of establishing action plans, but need to get back on track.

Have you been able to break down barriers and communicate more effectively as a result of this process? How or in what ways?

- Yes, by using the methods presented at the in-service.

- A little progress as far as coordinator to employee.

- Barriers have been broken down, but the team still has a few renegades and cliques.

- Co-workers, friends and family seem less defensive when things are worded right.

- How to deal with a difficult situation or co-worker.

How has this process been useful in helping you integrate and communicate with others on your team? Outside of your team?

- Working with persons outside the team, I've become more aware of what they are relating to me. I think more before I give an answer that may be an agitation to that person.

- It helped me to see there are two sides to everything and if you work together, there is always a solution that will benefit everyone.

- Very well; sometimes I surprise myself.

- It helps us break down barriers between union and management and lets us relate more to others.

- It provides a tool to give effective positive feedback.

- I wish I had heard this when my children were younger.

- Better listening, thinking things through more, better recall.

- By focusing on where the problems lie-within myself–where the attitude is coming from.

How has your behavior changed as a result of going through this process?

- Positively changed. More communicative, even with family.

- Positively changed. I don't self-destruct over criticism. I listen and evaluate info and don't over react or get emotional.

- Positively changed. I am more open to new ideas and change.

- Positively changed. I want to be open and honest to clear up a problem-and to find out if part of the problem was me–so I can try to improve to keep a better relationship with others.

- Positively changed. Tried to be more openly supportive of peers. Try to push (coach) support resources into being more available, open for feedback, etc.

- Positively changed. This has helped me to open up my thought process to others.

- Positively changed. More in tune with others' needs.

- Positively changed. I have a better understanding of how I sound to others and how to stay focused on the problem at hand.

- Positively changed. Cooperation, working together, everyone is more aware.

*What changes, recommendations or suggestions do you have
to improve this process?*

- None.

- I thought the program with Mike and Norm was great. I
  would not change anything, except to have all employees
  participate instead of only front-line people.

- Good program as it is.

- I wouldn't change anything-both Mike and Norm were
  terrific.

Other comments:

- I am more comfortable in seeking out my peers to ask for
  advice or support and camaraderie.

- I do understand that we all have different problems and ways
  to solve them.

- Although it was difficult initially to confront inappropriate
  behavior, it is becoming easier, due to better insight into those
  being confronted.

- It was helpful to see that my peers were struggling with the
  same issues as me; this helped to stimulate communication,
  gave us a basis for shared interest.

- It has been tough at times, but the group has been supportive
  of each other.

- Have received many notes of encouragement and direction
  and truly believe the climate is taking a change toward the
  positive.

- I have made a personal commitment and determined effort.
  I have focused energy in group dynamics, and not so much
  in individual support. I am not where I wish to be, but have
  made progress.

- The same principles apply in most any setting. Changing expectations of one another, leveling or confrontation in conflict, staying focused on the issue (not the person), taking risks, managing meetings-especially in a group of strong leaders.

- I think peers are more open-we are building trust.

- I have learned some new communication processes and how expectations play a part in the communication process.

- Better than other programs. I'm speaking only of team-building in this particular group. I believe that what I most appreciated was the facilitators' willingness to take risks. They promoted openness and honesty, with a strong sense of respectful behaviors for each participant. Although there could have been significant personal (business) risk, they behaved consistently with what was being asked of the rest of us.

- Better than other programs. This time the climate was right, with so much change in health care, we need to work together to keep our hospital provider of choice. Also, I feel you have "new guard" of managers that will work together and will take ownership.

- Better than other programs. Other programs did not focus on team building, I don't believe-i.e., no code of conduct established, risk-taking not encouraged.

- Better than other programs. Most honest sharing with members.

- Better than other programs. Mike and Norm are very good at this type of process. It's always a pleasure to work with them.

- Better than other programs. People didn't leave angry, and results came from the meetings. Helpful tools and ideas.

At a Midwestern medical center, results of an employee opinion survey indicated dissatisfaction and difficulties with the level and quality of communication between departments and co-workers and with dealing with conflict in the work environment. As a result, the medical center embarked on a five-month series of "Harnessing the Power of Conflict" workshops in which all employees were trained in communication skills, conflict resolution and mediation, using the Self-Mediation Process.

Following the program, staff reported significant improvement in every area of training given by the workshops.

- Employee relations had improved noticeably as a result of the mediation program.

- Positive attitudes regarding communications among departments and shifts improved after Harnessing the Power of Conflict training.

- Positive attitudes prevailed regarding peer work relationships within departments.

- Staff reported "cooperativeness" and "working well together" had significantly improved.

Here are some of the success stories that have occurred as a result of interventions using Harnessing the Power of Conflict:

- Focus factory supervisors began to communicate more effectively and to unify so that they could present a united front to their managers and not be perceived by the managers as disjointed, unorganized and too unruly to be effective.

- A union maintenance group worked more effectively together and overcame the problems of conflicting personalities and differing standards for three shifts.

- Helped nursing directors begin to work together to deal with problems and issues instead of making each other the enemy.

- Helped physicians to cooperate together as a team and to speak to each other and work to create better delivery of services.

- Assisted medical records department in moving on with self-directed work teams and to mediate differences without having to run to the supervisors.

- Helped a rehab nursing unit establish an effective code of conduct to ensure that all nurses on the unit live up to the standards and solve differences.

- Created peer mediation for the emergency services department of a hospital.

- One company instituted methods for resolving conflicts (before major conflicts occurred).

- Taught mediation methods as part of ongoing training techniques for line lead supervision.

- Helped a company's employees deal with each other, with management and ultimately with their board.

- Helped teach people how to interact effectively together as two major organizations merged together.

- Trained staff on how to teach this program to others.

A major Wisconsin health center reported that:

- 85 percent of participants learned constructive methods for dealing with problem people.

- 78 percent use and practice the techniques after the program.

Some of the participants said:

- I've effectively used the listening skills taught and am now able to identify needs when conflict arises.

- I am making opposing parties stay focused on the issues.

- I didn't think I was catching on, but this week I found myself using the techniques with a problem phone call from a family member. I was able to identify feelings, find out his needs, come up with an action he found helpful and prevent what could have been a frustrating interaction.

- I'm using mediation to listen and allow others to solve the problem. Now I try not to just give them a solution.

- I am being more sensitive to all the changes people go through when facing difficult issues.

- I've learned how to deal with my children.

Harnessing The Power of Conflict

ACKNOWLEDGEMENTS

The evolution and constant refinement of Harnessing the Power of Conflict took years of effort and assistance from a number of individuals, groups, systems and institutions that need to be recognized. Without all those involved, the feedback and occasional frustration, *Harnessing the Power of Conflict* would be a good program, but not the culture-changing process it is. At the risk of leaving someone unacknowledged, we would like to give credit and thanks to the following sources of inspiration.

First and most importantly we would like to give credit to our wives, Sandra Dasenbrook and Crystal Mastroianni and our children–Angela and Nick Mastroianni and Eliott, Jessica and Keith Dasenbrook–for their contribution and sacrifices to make this all possible. Much of what is presented in this book comes from our successes and challenges in trying to be good marriage partners and fathers. Our family support, especially when we would come home from traveling, helped us continue on the next day.

We also want to thank all of our clients who trusted us and our mediation process in working with their staff and organizations. It takes innovators and risk takers to first recognize that they have destructive conflict in an organization and then to try new approaches to old problems with the consistency to follow through. Our clients have had the wisdom to empower their staffs with the ability to solve their own problems. It was not always easy selling boards of directors, management and peers on this process given that we were promoting confrontation and asking employees just exactly what they thought!

Our co-workers and office staff were and continue to be a wealth of encouragement, giving us feedback, criticism and expertise. We are sure that at times we've been demanding, but they were able to be confrontational and compassionate. To them we say thanks, also.

Our thanks to Kathy Velasco, Leslie Roxworthy, Deb Strout, Sherry Young and Lincoln Brunner from Velasco and Associates for their help and guidance as editors and creative consultants. And thanks to Brian Thomas of Brian Thomas Photography for trying to make us look good in the portrait shots.

Lastly, we would like to thank those who went before us. We have not developed Harnessing the Power of Conflict in a vacuum. We have learned from such diverse fields as psychology, organizational development, marriage and family therapy, mediation and philosophy, as well as from simply trying to be good husbands, fathers and friends.

BIBLIOGRAPHY
The Self Mediation Method

Bartz, Wayner & Rasor, Richard A. *Surviving with Kids*. NY, Ballantine Books, 1978.

Bramson, Robert M. PhD. *Coping with Difficult People*. NY, Ballantine Books, 1981.

Burns, David D. MD. *Feeling Good: The New Mood Therapy*. NY, Avon Books, 1999.

Conner, Daryl R. *Managing at the Speed of Change*. NY, Villard Books, 1994.

Corsini, Raymond, ed. *Current Psychotherapies*. Itasca, IL, F.E. Peacock Publishers, Inc., 1973.

Covey, Stephen R. *The Seven Habits of Highly Effective People*. NY, Fireside Books, 1989.

Ellis, Albert Ph.D. *A Guide to Rational Living*. NY, Whilsire Books, 1997

Fisher, Roger & Ury, William. *Getting to Yes*. NY, Penguin Books, 1991.

Gladwell, Malcom. *The Tipping Point*. NY, Little Brown, 2000.

Fisher, Roger & Brown, Scott. *Getting Together*. NY, Penguin Books, 1988.

Gordon, Dr. Thomas. P.E.T. *Parent Effectiveness Training*. NY, Wyden, Inc., 1975.

Leadership Advantage. *The Business Case for Coaching*. 2001

Morin, William. Viewpoint: *Six Common Beliefs of Executives Who Fail*. Columns, Dec. 2002

Pastor, Larry M.D. "Single Session Therapy Effective in the Workplace." *Psychiatric Times*, Jul. 1993.

Ury, William. *Getting Past No*. NY, Bantam Books, 1993.

Weisinger, Hendrie. *Emotional Intelligence at Work*. San Francisco, Josey Bass, 1998.

Weiss, Donald. *Effective Team Building*. NY, Amacom (American Management Association), 1993.

Weiss, Donald. *Conflict Resolution*. NY, Amacom (American Management Association), 1993.

INDEX

Harnessing The Power of Conflict

The Self Mediation Method

EPILOGUE

EPILOGUE

A client of ours told this story to us, and we would like to end by sharing it with you.

In Korea, the farmers store their rice in huge ceramic bowls. Sometimes, a rat will get into the rice bowl. It is a foolish farmer who will take a stick and smash the bowl in order to remove the rat.

The moral of that story is simple. The rats can be symbols of problems we have on a team. We want to remove the problems, but we don't want to destroy the team and the entire structure to do so.

Harnessing the Power of Conflict helps to make sure that the problems are taken care of without destroying the whole team. What can happen is that a whole new vessel is created in the process. All of us want a team that functions well, and all of us want to be empowered and all of us want success. When we work cooperatively rather than adversely, all these things can be ours. Good luck with your attempts.